THE
ADOPTION
Answer Book

BRETTE MCWHORTER SEMBER

SPHINX® PUBLISHING
AN IMPRINT OF SOURCEBOOKS, INC.®
NAPERVILLE, ILLINOIS
www.SphinxLegal.com

First Edition: 2007

Published by: Sphinx® Publishing, An Imprint of Sourcebooks, Inc.®

Naperville Office
P.O. Box 4410
Naperville, Illinois 60567-4410
630-961-3900
Fax: 630-961-2168
www.sourcebooks.com
www.SphinxLegal.com

This publication is designed to provide accurate and authoritative information in regard to the subject matter covered. It is sold with the understanding that the publisher is not engaged in rendering legal, accounting, or other professional service. If legal advice or other expert assistance is required, the services of a competent professional person should be sought.

From a Declaration of Principles Jointly Adopted by a Committee of the American Bar Association and a Committee of Publishers and Associations

This product is not a substitute for legal advice.

Disclaimer required by Texas statutes.

Library of Congress Cataloging-in-Publication Data
Sember, Brette McWhorter, 1968-
  The adoption answer book / by Brette McWhorter Sember. -- 1st ed.
    p. cm.
  ISBN-13: 978-1-57248-607-2 (pbk. : alk. paper)
  ISBN-10: 1-57248-607-4 (pbk. : alk. paper)
  1. Adoption--United States. 2. Adoption--Law and legislation--United States. I. Title.

HV875.55.S45 2007
362.7340973--dc22
                                                                2007015207

Printed and bound in the United States of America.
VP — 10 9 8 7 6 5 4 3 2 1

Contents

Deciding to Adopt
Adoption and Fertility Treatments
Legal Effects
Birth Parents' Rights and Roles
Extended Birth Family
Legal Process
Adoption Support
Preparing for the Adoption Roller Coaster
Preparing for the Future

Open vs. Closed Adoption
Domestic vs. International Adoption
Agency vs. Private Adoption
Finding and Choosing an Agency
Finding and Choosing an Attorney
Facilitators
Affording Adoption

Home Studies
Consent
Adoption Court Procedures
Post Placement
Birth Certificates
Adoption Financial Credits

Taking Time Off for Your Adoption
Bonding with an Adopted Child
Dealing with Adoption Disappointments

Celebrating Your Adoption
Worrying about Your Adoption
Breastfeeding an Adopted Infant
Talking to Your Existing Children about Adoption
Raising Biological and Adopted Siblings
Talking to Your Adoptive Child about the Adoption
Keeping an Adoption a Secret
Cultural Heritage
Medical Issues
Post-Adoption Support
Finding Birth Parents

Introduction

Adoption is a very special and magical thing. A child is born to other people and becomes part of your family—legally, emotionally, and completely. Whether you are considering adoption or have already decided it is what you want, you probably have a lot of questions about the types of adoption available, the costs, and the procedures. This book is your legal and practical guide through all of the options before you.

If you are interested in adopting a U.S. child, you can work with a domestic public agency or a domestic private agency, or you can work with an adoption facilitator or locate a birth mother on your own. You may also be considering an international adoption, where you adopt a child from another country. If you are a stepparent, you may be interested in becoming your stepchild's legal parent through adoption. Foster parenting is an option that might appeal to you. Embryo donation/adoption and surrogacy are other methods of adding a child to your family using an adoption process that you may be considering. This book addresses all of these choices, and explains the processes and procedures you need to go through to bring your dream to reality.

Whether you are married, a straight single, a gay single, or part of a gay marriage or partnership, there are a wide variety of adoption opportunities for you to consider and pursue as you see fit. Adoption is considered by people who have children, have had unsuccessful fertility treatments, have never tried to have children, or who are currently undergoing fertility treatments. Whatever walk of life you are coming from, adoption is an option that can work for you.

While this book strives to give you the most up-to-date information available, laws are always changing, so you must always do your own research to make sure you get the most current information possible. It is also very important to consult an attorney experienced in adoption who can help you through the process and make sure you cross every "t" and dot every "i" so that your adoption goes smoothly and is done legally.

Adopting a child is one of the most wonderful journeys you will take in your life. Good luck on your journey.

Chapter 1

CHOOSING ADOPTION

Adoption is a wonderful way to create a family. Children who are adopted are children of their families just as much as biological children. In recent years, adoption has become less of a secret and more of a celebrated route to parenthood.

Deciding to Adopt

Making the decision to adopt is one that may have come to you easily, or after much difficulty. Some people come to the adoption process after unsuccessfully attempting to conceive a child themselves, with or without assisted reproduction treatments. Others simply know that adoption is the way for them to create or add to a family.

No matter how you got to this point, you are reading this book because you're interested in adopting a child. Adoption is not for everyone, and it is also important to remember that there is no one-size-fits-all adoption. There are many ways to adopt a child — internationally, through an agency, through a birth mother you find yourself, or when you adopt your stepchild. All types of adoption are important processes, and are choices that work for certain individuals.

There are a lot of issues to consider when you are looking into adoption. Not all of them are politically correct, but when it comes to making a decision that will affect the rest of your life, and your child's life, they are questions you must ask yourself. How comfortable would you be raising a child of a different race or color? How comfortable would you be raising a child who came from a background very different from yours? Would you be willing to raise a child who has disabilities? How do you feel about raising a child who is not related to you?

There are no right or wrong answers to these questions, only answers that work for you. Many parents worry that they won't love or bond with an adopted child, but if you talk with adoptive parents, you will find that they resoundingly tell you that they did so immediately, and that you will too. Adoption is not something strange or unnatural. It is simply another way to build a family. The answer to whether adoption is right for you is something you must discover in your own heart.

Adoption and Fertility Treatments

It is possible, and perfectly acceptable, to pursue adoption while undergoing fertility treatment. An adoption agency will not turn you away because you are undergoing fertility treatments. Many couples feel that adoption and assisted reproduction is an either-or proposition, but in fact many couples do explore and pursue both choices simultaneously. Because both processes can be long, it may make sense to consider both. Doing so also gives you more options. If you undergo *in vitro fertilization* (IVF) and begin the adoption process at the same time, you may decide to discontinue IVF in a few months if you're not successful, and your adoption process will be well underway. On the other hand, if you begin both and get pregnant through fertility treatments, you can stop your adoption process at that point. Some people find it is distracting to pursue both at the same time. This is a decision you must make for yourself, based on your own situation and feelings.

You and Your Partner

If you and your spouse or partner are on the same page about adoption, you're in a great position. However, it's not uncommon for couples to not always see eye to eye about how they want to start a family.

Sometimes one partner wants to try fertility treatments while another wants to try adoption. Before you can proceed with finding a child to adopt, you and your partner need to work together to find a solution you can both agree on. There is no doubt that the road to adoption is an emotional process, and you and your partner need to work through the various emotions and concerns together before you can move forward. If you find that you have difficulty reaching a consensus, some sessions with a couples counselor can help you both get to the root of your feelings and understand each other.

Legal Effects

When you are considering adoption, it is important to fully understand how the legal process works, and what effect the adoption legally has on your life.

When a child is adopted, the birth parents' legal ties to the child are completely severed. The child no longer has any legal connection to these parents. The adoptive parents become the child's legal parents. A new birth certificate is issued with the birth parents' names listed as the parents. An adopted child has the exact same rights as a couple's biological child in every way. Adopted children have the right to:

- inherit from their adoptive parent(s) and adoptive families;
- take their parents' last name(s);
- collect benefits (such as Social Security) through their parent(s); and,
- rely on their parent(s) for support.

Additionally, should a child's adoptive parents ever divorce, custody and visitation will be decided in the same way as it would for biological children. Being adopted has no impact on custody and visitation since an adopted child is legally no different from a child who is born to a couple. Even if the child is the biological child of one parent and is then adopted by the other parent, both parents have the same rights.

Adopted children also become legally related to the adoptive parents' extended family. For example, the adopted mother's mother is the child's legal grandmother. Adoptive children inherit from extended family just as a biological child would.

Birth Parents' Rights and Roles

When a child is born to a woman, she is legally the child's mother, unless and until a court issues an order stating otherwise. Birth fathers' rights are a little more slippery, simply because the identity of a child's biological father is not always obvious. If a woman is married when she gives birth, her husband is the legal father of the child, unless it is proven otherwise. If a woman is unmarried, a man can admit to being the father. There are two ways to admit paternity. One is to sign a document called an *admission of paternity*; the other is to sign a state registry called the *putative father registry*. Another way to have paternity determined is when a court issues an order determining paternity based on DNA testing.

When a child is adopted, both birth parents must *consent,* or agree, to the adoption (if the birth father is unknown or cannot be located, his consent is not needed). The adoption process allows both birth parents a period of time to change their minds about the adoption once the process is in motion. (See Chapter 3 for more information.)

Once the adoption process is finalized, the birth parents have no further legal rights to the child. They can never come back and decide they have changed their minds and want custody, and they do not have any right to see or spend time with the child. There are cases in which birth parents later challenge an adoption, but this is not the norm and only occurs when there is some kind of abnormality or problem in the way the adoption process was handled (for example, if one of the birth parents was not properly notified). It is important to understand that in most states, the birth parents have a period of time after the birth during which they can reconsider their consent to the adoption. This is not overturning the adoption; the adoption simply is not legal until this time period has ended. While this time period can be nerve-wracking, it is in place to make sure that parents give complete, knowledgeable consent to the adoption, because it is such an important process for everyone involved.

Extended Birth Family

Adoption also severs the child's legal ties to the birth parents' families — grandparents, aunts, uncles, cousins, and so on. The child is no longer legally related to these people, which means these people have no claim to visitation with the child. There are also no longer any inheritance rights. For example, if a grandmother leaves everything to be divided equally among her grandchildren, a child who was placed for adoption with another family no longer qualifies as one of her grandchildren. It is important to understand that adoption severs not only the rights of the birth family, but also their connection to the child. An adoption takes a child out of one family unit and places him or her into another. It is a complete and absolute substitution.

In some instances, however, a birth family continues to have contact with the child. It is becoming more common for a child to continue to have contact not only with birth parents, but also birth families. Despite the adoption, these people are a part of a child's history and even though the law changes their legal relationship, it is possible for them to continue to know each other. Often this is considered the healthiest way for an adoption to happen. You can change what a birth certificate says, but you cannot change a child's feelings. Continuing these family bonds can be important for older children who are adopted. This has to be done the right way, with the proper safeguards, so the child is not confused. (See Chapter 3 for more information.)

Legal Process

It is important to remember that the legal adoption process is separate from the process you will go through to find a child to adopt. Finding a child can take much longer and can involve choosing an agency, finding a birth mother on your own, or dealing with the requirements of the foreign country your child will come from. (See Chapter 5 for information about agencies; Chapter 7 about independent adoptions; and, Chapter 6 about international adoptions.) Many people face the legal process of adoption with some trepidation. Actually, the legal process is not that difficult. It is very clear cut and has a strict procedure to follow. A lot of the painful waiting involved in an adoption happens while you are trying to find a child to adopt. Once you have done that, the legal process is really a last hurdle and should not concern you greatly.

The legal process for adoption follows the same general path whether your adoption is a single-parent adoption, second-parent adoption, agency adoption, private adoption, or international adoption. The major components of the process include:

- a background check, where prospective parents are fingerprinted and have their backgrounds checked for criminal records;
- a home study, in which a social worker meets with the prospective parents and sees their home;
- the birth parents' consent to the adoption; and,
- the actual court procedure in which documents are submitted and reviewed, and the adoption is approved.

The legal process itself can take six months to a year. (See Chapter 3 for more information about the specific legal processes involved in adoption.)

Adoption Support

No matter what kind of adoption you are interested in, consider joining an adoption support group. (See Appendix A for more information.) These groups can provide practical information, contact information, support, and advice. Talking to other parents who have adopted or who are going through the adoption process will provide you with a clear perspective on how the process works and how it affects parents.

A support group is an excellent way to make connections, get information, hear other people's experiences, and consider new approaches. For example, you might only be considering an agency adoption, but through a support group you might learn of a birth mother interested in independent adoption and this may appeal to you. You will meet other couples seeking to adopt, as well as families who have successfully adopted. You may also meet attorneys and other adoption professionals who can assist you with your adoption journey. Some adoption support groups are specifically devoted to families who have adopted children from certain countries or areas, such as China. If you are interested in adopting from a specific country, locate one of these groups, online or locally, and talk with the members. You will be able to obtain very detailed information about what to expect.

If you are considering a second-parent adoption (in which a stepparent adopts the child of his or her spouse or partner, see Chapter 4 for more information), the decision process is a bit different since the child is already in your life. You are now confronting a legal decision, not a family-forming decision. This is a decision you must make with your partner or spouse and often with the child's input as well. Second-parent adoptions must also consider the child's other parent, if he or she is alive, since his or her consent will be necessary.

In addition to emotional support, it is helpful to have a resource to turn to for information. This book contains many websites and organizations that can help you. Perhaps the most important is your state *adoption specialist*. This office oversees all adoptions of foster care children and also maintains records and complaints about private agency adoptions. It is a good idea to check with this agency about any adoption agency you are considering. Contact information is contained in Appendix B.

Preparing for the Adoption Roller Coaster

No matter what kind of adoption you are considering or have selected, it is likely that the process will be emotional. Choosing to create a family is one of the most private decisions, yet when you choose to do so through adoption, suddenly there are social workers, lawyers, adoption case managers, and judges scrutinizing you, your life, your decision, your abilities, and your desirability. It can be disconcerting and frustrating to know that the future of your family rests in large part in the hands of these strangers. It also can be frustrating to realize that people who have biological children can have them without any approval or screening (and sometimes without even intention), but someone who desperately wants a child and wishes to adopt must go through an intrusive process.

Some adoption processes take longer and can be more difficult than others. If you are hoping to adopt a newborn in the United States, you must realize that finding a birth mother is a long and difficult process. If you are planning a second-parent adoption, you might be frustrated by the hoops that must be jumped through to make legal something that seems and feels obvious to you.

While waiting to adopt, it is important to have patience. Do everything you can to make the paperwork go smoothly. Never lose your belief that you will find your child.

While none of the adoption processes are as simple as sperm meeting egg, they are not as scary and drawn out as some people expect. Remember that the reward at the end is a child. That will make everything feel worthwhile.

Preparing for the Future

When you decide to adopt, your decision affects not only you and your partner, if you have one, but also your entire extended family. It also, of course, affects the child you bring into your family. Adoption is a decision that you may make today, but will affect the long-term future in many ways.

The type of adoption you choose will affect your child. If you use an agency adoption, your child will probably grow up with little or no contact with his or her birth parents. If you use independent adoption, it is likely your child will have some sort of contact with, or at least will know how to contact, his or her birth parents.

International adoption usually completely rules out most hope of your child having any contact with the birth parents. The results of any of these paths can have a long-term affect on you and your child, so it is important to consider every angle as you are making your decision.

> **Adoption Answer**
>
> Locate an adoption group in your area using this resource:
>
> **www.stateadoptions.com**

> **Adoption Answer**
>
> If you are considering adoption, take an adoption self-assessment to help you and your partner (if any) get a clear sense as to how you feel about the many choices available. One is available at:
>
> **http://adopting. adoption.com/child/ self-assessment-adoption- quiz.html**

Adoption Answer

Joining an adoption support group is an excellent way to get through the waiting. Consider joining an online group. The North American Council on Adoptable Children has a database of groups you can search at:

**www.nacac.org/pas_
database.html**

An adoption is a commitment to the future.

Chapter 2

ADOPTION DECISIONS

Once you have chosen to adopt, you will find that there are many more decisions ahead of you. You must choose:

- the type of adoption you are interested in;
- the people who will help you; and,
- what kind of relationship you want to have with the birth parents in the future.

Open vs. Closed Adoption

Adoptions used to be done in complete secrecy, with even the child being kept in the dark. Today, things have changed and most people are more honest about adoptions. Most adoptive children now grow up understanding that they were adopted, and many grow up knowing their birth mother. This concept of an *open adoption* is one in which the adoptive and birth parents have some contact (which can vary greatly) and the child knows that he or she is adopted. The child may even know or have contact with the birth parents. The degree of contact can range from minimal to very involved. For example, some adoptive parents see the birth mother frequently during the pregnancy, attend the birth, and continue to see her and have contact with her throughout the child's life. In other situations, an open adoption can mean that the adoptive parents meet the birth mother once, learn her first name, and obtain copies of her family medical history. A middle-of-the-road alternative includes some meetings or contact during pregnancy and photos and letters exchanged occasionally throughout the child's life.

The type of adoption you pursue will affect how open it is to some degree. *International adoptions* provide no contact with birth parents; *private adoptions* can be some of the most open; and, *domestic agency adoptions* can vary greatly depending on the agency's policies, your wishes, and the birth mother's wishes. Choosing an open or closed adoption depends on your personal feelings. It is important to understand that your adoption will not be specified as an open one or a closed one in your adoption papers. As far as the court is concerned, the adoptive parents become the legal parents and the birth parents have no further rights once the adoption is completed. The adoption legal process completely ends the birth parents' legal rights, but anything you choose to do from that point is up to you. It is important to realize that some birth mothers will not agree to the adoption if they do not feel you have made a commitment to the level of openness (or closure) they are seeking.

An important consideration in open adoption is how very real the baby and birth mother can be to you as you are waiting for the birth. This can be wonderful, because in a way you are included in the pregnancy process. It can also be heartbreaking if the birth mother ultimately decides not to go through with the adoption. Because you are so heavily invested in the situation and because the baby and birth mother are so much a part of your life, it can be emotionally very difficult to cope if the adoption is not completed.

An open adoption can also place more pressure on the adoptive parents. They must meet and be interviewed by the agency, by the social worker who does the home study, and sometimes by the birth mother. It can be very difficult to sit in a room with a woman who is carrying what might be your baby and try to measure up to whatever standards she is using. Some adoptive parents find that the relationship they carry on with the birth mother during the pregnancy can be emotionally draining. They feel they are on tiptoes the whole time, trying not to offend her and working hard to find the right level of involvement.

Some adoptive parents never feel quite sure how involved to get, what kind of help to offer, or even what to say at certain times. Your agency can help guide you through this process for the most part, but it is something to consider when you are deciding if you want an open adoption. Finally, some adoptive parents simply do not want the specter of the birth mother intruding on their lives. They do not want to meet or interact with her or think too much about her role or her connection to the baby once that child becomes theirs. Many adoptive parents worry she will exert some kind of emotional influence over the

> ### Adoption Answer
> You can read sample open adoption agreements online at:
>
> **www.findlaw.com**

> ### Adoption Answer
> For more information about open adoption, contact the American Association of Open Adoption Agencies at:
>
> **www.openadoption.org**

child and always be the *real* mother. These are individual decisions you must make on your own. As always, an adoption support group can help you through these thought processes and decisions.

Post-Adoption Agreements

Although an adoption is a final substitution in the child's legal family, many states now allow and enforce what are called *post-adoption agreements*. These agreements are between the adoptive parents and the birth parents or birth family and specify some kind of ongoing contact between the child and the birth parents or birth family. Currently, twenty-two states have laws that allow and enforce these agreements:

- Arizona
- California
- Connecticut (only when the child was adopted from foster care)
- Florida
- Indiana (only when the child is age 2 or older)
- Louisiana
- Maryland
- Massachusetts
- Minnesota
- Montana
- Nebraska (only when the child is adopted from foster care)
- Nevada
- New Hampshire
- New Mexico
- New York
- Oklahoma
- Oregon
- Rhode Island
- Texas
- Vermont (only in stepparent adoptions)
- Washington
- West Virginia

Post-adoption agreements must be approved by the court.

Domestic vs. International Adoption

Choosing between adopting a child within the United States (domestic adoption) or from another country (international adoption) is a common dilemma faced by potential adoptive parents. With domestic adoptions, it is generally easier to adopt a younger and possibly healthier child than from another country. However, international adoptions tend to be quicker and can be less costly.

The following two lists can help identify the pros and cons to each option. Choose the path that is most comfortable for you and your family.

Adoption Answer

Information to help you consider domestic vs. international adoption is available at:

www.adoptall.com/ intguide.html

Domestic Adoption

Pros:
- It is easier to adopt a newborn.
- The child is usually healthy and developmental delays are limited.
- You can obtain complete medical records for the baby.
- You can obtain a complete family medical history.
- Everything is conducted in English.
- You may be able to meet or have contact with the birth parents.
- The agency you are working with may be the one the child is placed through (which can simplify things).
- As complicated as the adoption process is, it is done only using the laws of this country and the requirements are very clear.
- If your child wants to meet his or her birth parents, it is at least possible.

Cons:
- This type of adoption generally takes a year or longer.
- You may have to wait longer to adopt a newborn, since there are very few available.

- You may have to deal with a birth mother who could change her mind after the baby is born.
- You may have to meet a birth mother's selection criteria.

International Adoption

Pros:
- These adoptions generally happen more quickly.
- There is no shortage of children available.
- The cost of the adoption is usually less than with domestic adoption.
- You gain not only a child but also an entire culture that becomes part of your family.

Cons:
- The child you adopt is usually no younger than three or four months old (newborns are not available because of the way the process works).
- Children may not be in good health and may have developmental delays.
- You may get little or no medical information about your child or his or her family.
- You will have the added expense of travel.
- The red tape you may need to deal with in your child's country of origin may be extensive.

Agency vs. Private Adoption

An *agency adoption* is one in which you work with an agency that will locate a child for you to adopt and provides most, if not all, the related services. Often, the birth parents give their consent to the adoption to the agency, and the agency then chooses the adoptive parents. Birth parents often have a say in agency adoptions, but often do not have complete control. In a *private adoption,* you locate a birth mother— through adoption attorneys, adoption facilitators, or on your own (often through word of mouth or by placing newspaper ads). However, many adoptive parents who do private adoptions use an agency to handle the adoption once the birth mother is located.

> ### Adoption Answer
> One of the most comprehensive and helpful resources available to parents seeking to adopt is the Child Welfare Information Gateway. Its website is almost certain to provide answers to almost any question you have. Find it at:
>
> **www.childwelfare.gov**

Some agencies can be difficult to work with, but when pursuing a private adoption, the entire process can be even more complicated. With each method having its own set of pros and cons, you must decide which one best suits your situation. Review the two lists on the following pages to help in your decision making.

Agency Adoption

Pros:
- The agency locates the child and does the legwork.
- The agency provides the social worker for the home study.
- The agency provides counseling and services.
- The agency is in charge of the adoption and moving it along.
- A good agency has plenty of children to adopt.
- The agency can help manage your relationship with the birth parents.

- The agency screens birth parents and usually chooses those less likely to change their minds.
- The search time may be shorter since the agency already has a network set up to locate birth mothers.
- The agency screens the adoptive parents and chooses those whom the birth parents will not object to.

Cons:
- The agency is in charge and things move at their pace, not yours.
- The agency can screen you out if they feel you are not desirable.
- You have no actual control over the process.
- You must pay agency fees in addition to other adoption expenses.
- An agency is an organization that does not always have your best interests as its main focus.
- You need to spend time locating the agency that is right for you.

Private Adoptions

Pros:
- You have control of the situation.
- You can develop the kind of relationship with the birth mother that feels right to you.
- You decide the pace at which the process moves.
- You can personally find and select a birth mother.
- You have more information about the birth parents.
- There are fewer people involved.
- There are no agency fees.
- You can immediately begin to bond with the child and can have extensive contact with the birth mother during the pregnancy.

Cons:

- The process can be riskier, with the birth mother more likely to change her mind.
- You may need to spend a lot of time searching or advertising for birth mothers.
- You do not have as many professionals guiding you and supporting you.
- You are responsible for understanding the laws of your state or finding an attorney to guide you as you look for birth mothers.
- The costs are more unpredictable.
- You cannot select the gender of the child—whatever your birth mother has, you get.
- It can be more stressful than going through an agency.

Finding and Choosing an Agency

If you choose to work with an agency to adopt, it will be important to take some time to interview several agencies and choose the one that you are most comfortable with and confident in. You will be paying the agency a lot of money and you want to make sure that you get the results you want. If you are seeking to do an international adoption or a domestic adoption (which is not a private adoption or a second-parent adoption), you will have to use an agency. Agencies can be profit or nonprofit, but both still charge fees. Agencies may be public (run by the state) or private (run by a private company). Agencies can also be religious or nonsectarian, but it is important to know that most religious-based agencies do not require adoptive parents to be members of that religion.

An agency cannot reject you because of race or religion. However, marital status can be used as a determining factor, as can sexual orientation. The best way to locate an agency is by word of mouth, through adoption support groups, or through people you know who have used an agency successfully. Once you have a few names of agencies to consider, make an initial phone call and request information by mail. If the agency has a website, be sure to visit it. Many agencies provide informational meetings you can attend to learn more about the agency as well as the adoption process. Do not sign up with any agency before you have time to ask questions, compare it to others, and think about the decision. Ask about informational meetings and be sure to attend them. Ask questions and be observant. If you still feel the agency is a possibility, schedule an interview and use the questionnaire beginning on page 26 to evaluate and record responses.

One thing you will need to get a clear picture of is the agency's fee. The agency will collect fees to cover the home study, application, birth mother's expenses (if it is a domestic adoption), and other costs. Some agencies will clearly enunciate these separate amounts for you. Be wary of an agency that lumps total costs together and will not provide a breakdown. Call your state's agency that licenses and monitors adoption agencies (your social services or family and children department) and ask for information about the adoption agency, including its history and any complaints that have been filed against it. Ask to speak to an adoption specialist in the department and question the agency's reputation. The average length of time for an adoption should be under two years. If an agency has a longer average, you may want to go somewhere else. When you have chosen an agency, make sure you get everything in writing so there can be no confusion or dispute. You will need to sign a contract with the agency that will spell out the fees, procedures, and responsibilities.

Finding and Choosing an Attorney

No matter what type of adoption you choose to pursue, you will need an attorney to represent you. It is important to select an attorney who is experienced in handling adoptions. If you have an attorney you have used for other matters, ask him or her for a referral. Ask members of your adoption support group for referrals. You can also call your state or city bar association and ask for a referral. Once you have some attorneys to consider, schedule a free consultation. Use the *Attorney Evaluation Questionnaire* on page 28 to help you evaluate the

attorney. Make sure you get a clear picture of the attorney's fees. If you are seeking a private adoption, you will need to find out if the attorney is able to help you locate birth mothers or if he or she will only handle the legal paperwork. Expect attorney fees to range from $2,000 to $7,000, depending on the type of adoption and where you live. Avoid attorneys who seek *contingency fees* (paid only if they accomplish certain things such as finding a child for you to adopt). This can motivate an attorney to use unethical means to find a child for you to adopt. Make sure that when you do select an attorney, your agreement with him or her is in writing and is in the form of a retainer agreement or retainer letter.

> **Adoption Answer**
>
> For a referral to an attorney, contact:
>
> **American Academy of Adoption Attorneys**
> P.O. Box 33053
> Washington, DC 20033
> 202-832-2222
> **www.adoption**
>
> **attorneys.org**

Facilitators

Adoption *facilitators* are professionals who locate birth mothers for adoptive parents. They can play an ongoing role throughout the adoption process and take on a coordinating position similar to that an agency plays. Be aware that many states do not permit the use of adoption facilitators. Some states do permit facilitators to operate, but do not license or regulate them. (California does license facilitators and Pennsylvania legally recognizes them as well.) Be sure to talk to your attorney about the legalities of using a facilitator. Also, be certain to check references and backgrounds of any facilitators you consider. Do not work with anyone without a contract and make sure that your attorney approves the contract.

The following states do not permit paid adoption facilitators:

- Colorado
- Florida
- Georgia
- Kentucky
- Maryland
- Missouri
- New Jersey
- New York
- Oklahoma
- Oregon
- Tennessee
- Virginia
- West Virginia

It is important to distinguish between paid and unpaid facilitators. Many adoptions happen through *unpaid facilitators*. A minister, doctor, therapist, or nurse might work with a woman who is pregnant and help her find an agency or an adoptive family. These facilitators are doing nothing wrong. However, many states object to *paid facilitators*. Part of the problem is that these kinds of facilitators fall outside the specific requirements that states place on adoption agencies and can operate on their own. There may come a time when all states will license, regulate, and allow facilitators, but for now, you must be very clear about what your state permits and does not permit. If you can use a facilitator, the advantage is that the relationship is more personal than with an agency. He or she personally (for the most part) handles the details of your adoption and is personally accountable to you. The downside is that in most states, a facilitator is not licensed or regulated and operates completely on his or her own, with no safeguards for adoptive families and no required training.

There are also facilitators who handle international adoptions. In general, this is not recommended (the U.S. Department of State specifically advises parents against it) since it does not give you the same level of protection that a well-known agency does.

Affording Adoption

When considering adoption, many people are taken aback by the costs involved. It can be particularly difficult to accept the costs if you are adopting a special needs child. The type of adoption you are using will directly affect the cost to you and some alternatives are more affordable than others. Following are estimates for the costs of different types of adoptions.

- Foster Care Adoptions $0–$2,500
- Licensed Private Agency Adoptions $5,000–$40,000+
- Independent Adoptions $8,000–$40,000+
- Facilitated/Unlicensed Adoptions $5,000–$40,000+
- International Adoptions $7,000–$30,000

All adoptions have the following expenses:
- Home study: $1,000–$3,000
- Legal fees: $500–$12,000

Other expenses that your adoption may include are:
- travel, either interstate or internationally;
- counseling fees for the birth mother and yourself;
- agency fees;
- advertising;

- training classes;
- medical costs;
- interpreters and translators;
- escort fees;
- passport fees;
- gifts; and,
- document preparation.

Despite these expenses, affording adoption can be easier than you think. Once you have adopted a child, you are eligible for federal and state tax credits to reimburse you for expenses. (See Chapter 3 for more information.) There are additional funds for people who adopt special needs children. Many employers offer adoption cost partial reimbursement programs. Thirty-six percent of the 936 largest U.S. employers provide reimbursement programs, with the average reimbursement being $3,879, according to a Hewitt survey. Talk to your human resources department for information about this.

> **Adoption Answer**
>
> For more information on state laws about facilitators and other adoption laws, visit:
>
> **www.theadoption guide.com**

You may also wish to consider purchasing *adoption insurance.* It will reimburse you for expenses if a planned adoption does not take place. Adoption insurance can be difficult to locate, but one source is Heffernan/MBO Insurance Brokers in Menlo Park, California (800-833-7337). You might also talk to an insurance broker in your area. However, these types of insurance policies often only apply if you work with agencies or attorneys on the list approved by the insurance carrier.

The National Adoption Foundation has $9 million in revolving loans available to adoptive parents. Some of these loans are *unsecured loans,* meaning you do not put up any security, such as a house, to guarantee the loan. They also offer home equity loans in which your home is used as security for the loan. The loans typically average $2,500 and are financed through MBNA bank.

Adoption Answer

For more information about adoption insurance, contact:

National Adoption Foundation
100 Mill Plain Road
Danbury, CT 06811
203-791-3811
www.nafadopt.org

Adoption can be expensive, but it is not completely out of reach for most families. If you are considering adoption, you may wish to create a separate bank account and start saving what you can to help pay for the costs. Look into the special adoption loans available or consider a home equity loan through your own bank. You might also consider letting family and friends know you are saving for adoption and ask for contributions to your fund instead of holiday or birthday gifts.

If you are planning to add a child to your family, you already know that the child will bring added expenses. The money you earn now will have to stretch further to accommodate a child's needs. You can make adoption affordable by beginning to act like parents now—take the money it would cost to raise a child each week or each month and set that aside to help pay for the adoption.

Another consideration is comparing adoption expenses with assisted reproduction treatment expenses. The cost of adopting a child may turn out to be a lot less than pursuing months of unsuccessful fertility treatments. This is a choice you must weigh on your own, since obviously money is not the only consideration when choosing how you will add a child to your family.

Agency Evaluation Questionnaire

Name of Agency _____

Name of Contact Person _____

Date of Interview _____

Questions:
- Are you licensed in this state?
- How long have you been in business?
- Can you provide references?
- Do you handle domestic or international adoptions?
- If both, which do you place more often?
- Can you place children from other states?
- Do you have religious restrictions?
- What other guidelines or restrictions do you have in place?
- What is your fee structure?
- Can you provide a fee breakdown?
- When are the amounts due?
- What fees are not included in this?
- What is the average length of time for one of your adoptions?
- How many placements do you make per year?
- What is your percent of placements versus failed adoptions?
- How many in the last year?
- How many people are on your waiting list to adopt?
- Do you have infants available?
- What is the average age of the children placed through your agency?
- What portion of fees are refundable if the adoption does not occur?
- Please explain your home study process.
- How long does your average adoption take?
- Can you provide a list of approved social workers to use for the home study?

- Will you assist with a private adoption?
- What fees would apply?
- How are your birth mothers located?
- Who makes the placement decision—the agency or the birth mother?
- How is placement decided?
- What is your position on open adoption?
- What kind of relationship do you encourage or advise for birth parents and adoptive parents?
- Do you provide counseling for birth and adoptive parents?
- Are there additional fees for this?
- What is involved in the counseling process?
- What medical history information is provided to adoptive parents about the birth parents?
- Are birth mothers screened for HIV and other conditions?
- Do you give random drug tests to birth mothers?
- If potential adoptive parents turn down a birth mother, may they continue in the program and receive the next available placement?
- If an adoption is not completed, can the expenses be transferred or rolled over to a new birth mother?
- What other services does the agency provide?
- What is your policy on divorce, singles, and families with biological children?
- Do you have a grievance policy?
- If so, how does it work?
- If not, how are problems resolved?

Attorney Evaluation Questionnaire

Name of Firm _____

Name of Attorney _____

Date of Interview _____

Questions:
- How long have you practiced adoption law?
- What states are you licensed in?
- How many adoptions do you handle per year?
- How many have you handled in the last six months?
- Do you handle domestic or international adoptions or both?
- What percent of your practice is made up of these two types?
- Do you handle private adoptions?
- How many have you handled?
- What role do you take in the private adoption process?
- What are your fees?
- Do you charge a flat fee or an hourly rate?
- What kind of payment schedule do you use?
- Can you recommend any agencies that you have worked with in the past?
- How long does the average adoption process take?

Chapter 3

ADOPTION PROCEDURES

While there are a variety of different types of adoption to consider and choose from, some things are common to all the choices. You will need a home study; you will need to understand the issues of consent and revocation of consent by birth parents; and, you will face a court procedure to finalize the adoption. This chapter provides an overview of these considerations and procedures. Later chapters will discuss specifics that apply to each different type of adoption.

Home Studies

A *home study* is an evaluation and investigation of prospective parents' histories, backgrounds, home, finances, lifestyle, and parenting abilities. Home studies are required in almost all adoptions, but in some states they may be waived for second-parent adoptions. (See Chapter 4 for more information.)

A home study is done by a licensed *social worker.* If you work with an agency, the agency may have a list of social workers it works with or may have social workers who are employed by the agency. If you are doing an independent adoption, you will need to find a social worker yourself who can do a home study. Make sure that the social worker you use is licensed in your state.

The home study is probably the most feared hurdle in the adoption process by many prospective parents. In reality, it is not nearly as terrifying as it may sound.

A social worker will come to your home, meet you and your spouse (if you have one), and ask you questions about your background. These questions can cover information such as:

- where you were born;
- your family;
- your finances;
- your education;
- your health;
- your job history;
- any previous marriages;
- any previous addresses;
- any arrests or convictions; and,
- other children you have.

The social worker will also ask questions about your lifestyle and personal life. These questions can cover topics including:

- your employment schedule;
- income;
- friends and family you spend time with;
- organizations you belong to;
- pets;
- religious beliefs;
- hobbies and interests;
- smoking, drinking, and drug use;
- medical conditions;
- infertility and any treatments you have undergone or are undergoing;
- why you want to adopt;
- how you plan to make room in your life for a child;
- where the child will sleep;
- child care plans;

- how you will discipline a child; and,
- how you will adjust your finances to include a child.

There is no right answer to any of these questions. The most important thing you can do is be honest. Dishonesty is the biggest mistake you can make because it will usually be discovered and then the social worker and agency will have to wonder why you lied or what else you were not honest about.

In general, the purpose of the questions is to find out if you have a stable lifestyle; if you would be able to raise a child; if you have a support network in place (i.e., family and friends); if you are financially stable

Adoption Answer

See a sample adoption home study online at:

www.1-800-homestudy.com/homestudy/sample

and can support a child; if your home is conducive to a child; and, if you can emotionally handle being a parent. No parent is perfect, so no one is going to expect you to present a perfect picture of yourself. You can prepare yourself for these questions by simply reading over the list of questions and thinking about what you might say. It is a mistake to prepare a script for yourself—to recite answers you have planned and memorized—but thinking through the questions in advance and coming up with some general ideas about how you will respond can make you feel more comfortable.

The social worker will want to see your home and will be particularly interested in where the child will sleep. Your home does not have to be spotless and it does not have to be childproof. However, it is a good idea to show that you understand the basics of childproofing and explain how you will make the home safe for a child. You may need to meet with the social worker more than once to cover all the information that is needed. Do not become overwhelmed by this process. Some prospective parents spend weeks repainting the house and decorating a nursery. Doing so may make you seem a little overanxious, but it is certainly nothing the social worker has not seen before. Your home should simply be relatively clean and neat. This is not a contest to decide who would be the best parent. The home study is simply a way of making sure you are a decent person who is able to care for a child. The standards are really not as high as you might worry.

Additionally, you will be asked to write an autobiographical statement that will probably reiterate the information you provide verbally. This statement is brief — just a page or two — and should include information about why you want to adopt, as well as a brief history of your life. You will need to provide certified copies of birth and marriage certificates (as well as divorce decrees if applicable) and a medical report from your physician describing your health and explaining any conditions you have. You will also need written verification of your income (pay stubs or tax returns). Another part of the home study is providing references — three to five people who know you well and can say nice things about you. This should include a variety of people, such as friends, neighbors, clergy, coworkers, employers, and so on. They will be asked to provide letters explaining how they know you, how long they have known you, and why they believe you would make good adoptive parents.

Choose people who know you well. It would look strange to get a reference from someone who has only known you a short while. Select people who are themselves upstanding members of the community. It is always a good idea to include a reference from a minister, rabbi, or priest if you are involved in a church or temple. (It is okay if you are not religious and there is no need to join a church or temple just so you can get a letter of reference.)

In general, it is a good idea to choose people who have some kind of status — people with respected jobs, such as teachers, lawyers, business owners, and so on. While a good friend who is an exotic dancer may know you well and have wonderful things to say about you, a letter from someone else who knows you well and has a more respected profession is probably going to look better. However, always remember to stick to people who know you well — that is more important than any status.

You will also need to be fingerprinted and/or have a criminal background check done. If your state requires fingerprints, you will be given a card or paperwork and be told to go to your local police station to be fingerprinted. A background check requires you to complete a form with your name, address, and Social Security number. This is then run through a computer to check for convictions, child abuse problems, or outstanding warrants.

If you have been arrested or convicted of a crime in the past, all is not lost. The *Adoption and Safe Families Act* is a federal law that specifies which crimes states should screen for. Each state can opt out of these requirements and create their own, so it is important to check your state laws for specific information. In general, you are prohibited from adopting if you have been convicted (not just arrested) for any of the following.

- crimes against children:
  - child abuse
  - child neglect
- felonies:
  - spousal abuse
  - crime against a child (such as child pornography)
  - rape
  - sexual assault
  - homicide
- felonies in the past five years:
  - physical assault
  - battery
- drug-related offenses

NOTE: *If you have a past drug conviction for something like possession, it will be important to show that you went to rehab and you may wish to include a letter from a sponsor, rehab counselor, or someone else involved in your recovery so that there is reassurance that you have recovered and moved on with your life.*

Keep in mind that there is generally a separate fee for the home study (which can range from $1,000 to $3,000). If you are working with an agency, this may not be included in the agency fees.

Once you have jumped through all the required hoops, the social worker will write up a report that describes you and includes a recommendation as to whether or not you should adopt. The entire home study process can take anywhere from a few weeks to a few months, depending on how quickly things can be scheduled. Ask to receive a copy of the complete home study. The home study will be valid for either a year or eighteen months. Most adoptions can be completed within that time frame. If your adoption is not, all you need to do is have the home study updated, which is a much less complicated process and usually involves just one meeting with the social worker to make sure all your information is still accurate.

Consent

All adoptions involve some form of *consent*—agreement by the birth parents that the child should be adopted. If there are no living birth parents or the child was abandoned, then consent must be given by the state or country where the child is a resident. Consent is the biggest and most important hurdle to adoption. Procedures are in place to make sure birth parents are given adequate time to make their decision.

The type of consent required varies in each state, and in each country. The birth parents must sign a document in which they consent to the adoption and agree to give up all their rights to the child. In many states, the birth parents must also appear before a judge and verbally agree to the consent. Some states have the birth mother file a paper with the court called a *petition of relinquishment.* The birth mother can only give consent after the birth of the child, while the birth father can consent before birth. The thinking is that birth mothers often feel different after they have given birth to and have seen their child. (See the chart starting on page 36 for complete details on consent laws.)

The birth mother must always provide consent to the adoption. The birth father must also provide consent, if *paternity* has been established. Paternity can be established through an *admission* by the father or through a court proceeding. Many states also have what is called a *putative father registry.* This is a place where a man can register if he believes he is the father of a child. Before a child is placed for adoption, the putative father registry must be searched. If someone has registered, paternity will be tested.

Birth Fathers

Fathers' rights are an area of growing concern in the legal community. The problem with fathers' rights is that a birth father often does not know that he has fathered a child and the adoption happens without his knowledge or consent. The putative father registry helps with this issue, but does not completely alleviate it, since if a man has no idea that a woman he was involved with became pregnant, he has no reason to register. Most men do not register every sexual encounter they have.

The *Baby Richard* case that occurred in Illinois is one many people think of when they think about the issue of fathers' rights. What many people do not understand about that case is that the birth mother lied to the birth father and told him the baby had died at birth, when instead she placed the baby for adoption. He later discovered the lie and eventually gained custody of the child who was, by that time, four years old. The birth mother also attempted to revoke her consent to the adoption. This case had components most cases do not—the marriage between the birth parents and the lie that was told.

Although the *Baby Richard* case is one that is unlikely to be repeated, it is a good example of why it is important to have consent from both birth parents whenever possible. In some instances that is not possible—and if your attorney is comfortable with the situation, then you should feel comfortable as well.

Older Children

In most states, older children who are adopted must give their consent. The age varies from state to state:

age 10:

- Alaska
- Arkansas
- Hawaii
- Maryland
- New Jersey
- New Mexico
- North Dakota

age 12:

- Arizona
- California
- Colorado
- Connecticut
- Florida
- Idaho
- Kentucky
- Massachusetts
- Montana
- New Hampshire
- North Carolina
- Ohio
- Oklahoma
- Pennsylvania
- South Dakota
- Texas
- Utah
- West Virginia

age 14:

- Alabama
- Delaware
- District of Columbia
- Georgia
- Illinois
- Indiana
- Iowa
- Kansas
- Maine
- Michigan
- Minnesota
- Mississippi
- Missouri
- Nebraska
- Nevada
- New York
- Oregon
- Rhode Island
- South Carolina
- Vermont
- Virginia
- Washington
- Wyoming

A child's consent is not required:

- Louisiana
- Tennessee
- Wisconsin

No Consent Needed

Consent is not needed if the birth parent has *abandoned* the child, had his or her rights *terminated* by the state (usually through an abuse or neglect proceeding in which the child is placed in foster care and then eventually freed for adoption), is *dead,* or if there are *special circumstances,* such as failure of the parent to have contact with the child for a lengthy period of time. These situations normally occur when a child is in foster care and the state has terminated the parental rights. There are instances when a child can be placed for adoption by a birth mother and no consent will be needed from the birth father, if he has abandoned the child or had no contact with the child for a certain period of time, as specified in your state's adoption laws.

When no consent is needed from the birth parents, the procedure seems as if it should go more quickly, but in reality it usually takes the same period of time. Adoptions are time consuming because of the amount of paperwork that must be processed about the adoptive parents and because many families are waiting to find a child to adopt. The consent process does not add that much time to the process. At the most it may add a month or two if there is an extended period after birth during which the birth mother can change her mind.

Notice

In some cases, the birth father may not be part of the child's life or may not be able to be located. In instances that this occurs, the court will allow *notice* to be given to him. This can include sending certified letters or court documents to his last known address or workplace, or publishing a notice in a newspaper selected by the court. If the father does not respond, he is presumed to have waived his right to oppose the adoption. If notice is required in your adoption, your attorney will take careful steps to make sure it is done correctly. If notice is not given properly, the birth father could later come back and seek custody. If notice is given properly and the birth father does not respond, his rights are terminated. Once parental rights are terminated, they can only be changed by showing that the proper procedure was not followed. If your state notice laws are carefully followed, there should not be problems with a birth father coming back later and trying to contest the adoption.

Timing of Consent

Birth fathers can give consent to adoption at any time. However, there are specific time frames in which a birth mother can give consent and have it be valid. This is usually only after the child is born. Alabama and Hawaii allow consent beforehand, but require a *reaffirmation* after the birth. There is usually a waiting period between the birth and when the birth mother's consent becomes final, and that can vary from twelve hours after the birth to fifteen days afterwards.

Consent Procedures

Birth parent consent can be done in writing (usually notarized) in some states. Other states require that it be done in court—either by appearing before the judge or by filing certain court papers. The birth parent must indicate that he or she understands the ramifications of what he or she is doing and willingly gives up all rights to the child. The consent procedure is very simple when it occurs in court. The adoption case is scheduled for a court appearance. The birth mother appears and simply tells the court she consents to the adoption. The judge makes sure she understands exactly what she is agreeing to and that she is agreeing to it of her own volition. There is no trial or complicated hearing involved. In most cases, if there is a problem with consent (i.e., the birth mother has changed her mind and does not want to give it), you will know about it in advance. It is very rare that a birth mother walks into a courtroom and drops a bombshell.

Revocation

Revocation is the withdrawal of consent by a birth parent after he or she has given legal consent and the adoption has started to go forward. Everyone who is looking to adopt has heard horror stories about adoptions being revoked at the last minute. Revocation is actually difficult to do. A few states do not allow any revocation under any circumstances. Others permit revocation only if there has been fraud, coercion, or other factors that indicate that the birth parent did not have complete knowledge or free will at the time of the consent. A few states allow birth parents to change their minds for any reason within a certain time period. If a birth mother revokes her consent in these states, the adoption does not occur. Usually, if there is an agency involved, there will be last-minute negotiations to try to complete the adoption, but by law, once a birth mother changes her mind, the adoptive family has no rights. The child is not theirs until the adoption is finalized and the adoption is not finalized without the completion of the consent.

While it is a sad thing to have happen, it is a possibility that all adoptive families must confront. The good news is that most birth mothers do not try to revoke their consent. To avoid a consent problem, it is important that the birth mother receive counseling during and after the pregnancy. It is also important that adoptive parents pursue only those adoptions that they have good feelings about and that seem likely to go through. If an adoption does fall through, you must know that it is not your fault and there is nothing you could have done to change the situation, as heartbreaking as it may be. You would not want to adopt a child knowing that you are taking him or her away from the birth mother against her will. Even if you believe that you can provide a better home for the child, you must accept the fact that the birth mother has the absolute right to keep her child if she so decides within the period of time allowed in your state. Once the court has finalized the adoption, there is no possibility that the adoption can be revoked. (Court proceedings are discussed later in this chapter.)

The following lists discuss when revocation is allowed and the time periods after consent for revocation in each state.

No revocation allowed (unless fraud, duress, etc.):
- Arizona
- California (agency adoption)
- Colorado
- Florida (if adoptive parents are identified)
- Kansas
- Mississippi
- Nebraska
- New Hampshire
- New Jersey
- New Mexico
- Oklahoma
- Oregon
- South Carolina
- Utah
- West Virginia
- Wisconsin
- Wyoming

No revocation at all (unless in the child's best interest):
- Hawaii
- Indiana
- Louisiana (birth fathers only)
- Massachusetts
- Nevada
- New York (private adoption)
- North Dakota
- Ohio
- Rhode Island

Three days:
- Florida (if adoptive parents not identified)
- Illinois
- Maine
- North Carolina (unborn infants and infants under three months of age)

Four days:
- Iowa

Five days (after birth):
- Louisiana

Seven days:
- North Carolina

Ten days:
- Alaska
- Arkansas
- District of Columbia
- Georgia
- Minnesota
- Tennessee

Fourteen days:
- Alabama

Fifteen days:
- Oklahoma (out-of-court consents only)
- Virginia

Twenty days:
- Kentucky

Twenty-one days:
- Vermont

Thirty days:
- California (direct placement)
- Maryland

Forty-five days:
- New York (consent made outside of court)

Sixty days:
- Delaware

Any time before final decree:
- Connecticut
- Idaho
- Michigan
- Missouri
- Montana
- Pennsylvania
- South Dakota
  (final decree takes two years)
- Washington

Adoptive Parent Consent

It is also important to understand that the adoptive parents must give their consent to the adoption. You can change your mind any time until the adoption is finalized by the court. This is something very few adoptive families consider, but it is important to understand your rights. Just because you say you want to adopt a child, you are not obligated to do so. It is your right to decide who you will bring into your family and how that will happen. You have no formal commitment to anyone until the adoption has been legally finalized. However, if you change your mind, you cannot get a refund on the expenses you have paid. If you adopt a child and later determine that the situation is not going to work, you cannot just give the child back. You would need to have your parental rights terminated by the state and you would also probably be required to pay for the expenses of foster care up until termination.

Adoption Court Procedures

The actual court procedure for an adoption is the last big hurdle in the process. As previously discussed, revocation of consent is the only real worry facing prospective adoptive parents at this point.

Your adoption will be handled in your state's family, juvenile, or surrogate's court. Your attorney will file your adoption petition and other paperwork. The court will review all the documents, including the home study and background checks. If the birth parents are required to or choose to give consent in front of the judge, this will happen in the courtroom.

If the child is of the age set by the state, he or she will be asked to consent to the adoption. If a birth father could not be located and notice was given, the court will review the notice to make sure it meets the state's requirements. The adoptive parents may appear in court to tell the judge they agree to the adoption. The adoption is then finalized and the judge signs the final order. This makes it official and legal. There is no testimony, cross-examination, or other courtroom theatrics. Adoption procedures are quiet and simple. There are legalities that must be taken care of, but by the time you go to court to finalize the adoption, all problems should be behind you. Once you have dealt with the consent issues, your adoption is usually very simple.

Adoption proceedings are happy occasions and judges are usually pleased to be part of them. Judges spend most of their time dealing with cases where people are arguing or are unhappy, so it is a pleasant experience for them to handle a case where the result is a happy ending. Most judges will allow family and friends to join you in the courtroom. The court staff will often congratulate the adoptive parents and "ooh" and "ahh" over the adoptive child. When the adoptive child is old enough to speak and understand what is happening, he or she is often made a part of the proceeding as well and is made to feel as if something very special has happened for him or her. Some judges will even give the child a certificate or a card in further recognition of how special the event is. If you wish to take photographs or videos, be sure to check with the court staff beforehand.

Post Placement

With most agency adoptions, you will have some *post placement* contact with the agency or with a social worker. You may have one or two post placement visits from the social worker to make sure things are going smoothly and to offer some assistance with adjustments. These visits are usually nothing to worry about. The worker is not going to rip your child from your arms and take him or her back. The worker will prepare a post placement report that is filed with the agency and may be filed with the court if required in your state.

Sometimes a child is placed with you before the adoption is finalized. This is particularly common in state public agency adoptions. If you are the child's foster parent and are adopting him or her, he or she would also already be living with you. In these cases, post placement visits happen after the child is placed with you and before the adoption occurs to make sure things are going smoothly. In general, they are nothing to worry about for the average parent.

Post placement visits are not about determining if the adoption should be allowed. They are about making sure you have support and helping the agency see that it went well. Post placement visits cannot undo an adoption; however, if a worker notices a child is being neglected or abused, it could open up a court procedure to deal with the situation.

Once your state has finalized and legalized your adoption, you have nothing to worry about unless a post placement visit is required before finalization in your state.

Birth Certificates

After the adoption is finalized, you need to get an amended birth certificate for your adopted child. Your attorney will request this form. The new birth certificate will list the adoptive parents as the child's legal parents, but maintain the child's actual birth date. This will be your child's official, legal birth certificate. The old birth certificate still exists as a state record, but it is not accessible. The adoption court proceeding also becomes sealed and not accessible. This is why you hear about adult adoptees having difficulty finding their birth parents. The information about the birth becomes inaccessible to protect privacy.

If you are interested in an adoption in which information about the birth parents is accessible to the child, see Chapter 2.

Adoption Financial Credits

Once you adopt, under the *Hope for Children Act,* you are entitled to up to a $10,630 deduction (as of the time this book was published) for the expenses associated with your adoption that you have not been reimbursed for on your income tax return. If you adopt a special needs child, you are entitled to the full deduction (with some income restrictions) without having to show expenses. You need to use IRS Form 8839 to claim the credit (see your tax preparer for more details). Additionally, if you cannot take the full deduction, you can *carry forward* (take in later years) the remaining amounts. Talk to your accountant or tax preparer about this credit. (Second-parent adoptions and surrogacy do not qualify.) Additionally, once your child has been adopted, you can list him or her as a dependent on your federal taxes, so make sure you let your tax preparer know about the adoption. Some states also offer adoption tax credits, so inquire about this. Once you are a parent, there are other child-related tax breaks available, including deductions for child care. Sit down with your tax preparer and find out how you can best approach taxes as a new parent. Many employers offer adoption expense reimbursement. Check with your human resource manager to find out if your company offers such a program. Employer assistance is not taxed, so this is yet another tax break.

Family Leave

The federal *Family and Medical Leave Act* allows parents to take unpaid time off from work to care for a newly adopted child (as well as ill family members and for the birth of biological children) within the first twelve months after adoption of the child.

You must work for an employer with at least fifty employees and you must have been employed at least twelve months and worked at least 1,250 hours. You can take up to twelve total weeks of leave in a twelve-month period. If you and your spouse work for the same employer, you are only given twelve weeks total between you to split. You can take all the leave at once or spread the leave out so that you work some or all of the time on a part-time basis. When possible, you must give thirty days' notice of the leave. When you return to work, your employer must reinstate you to your job or to a similar position. Some states also have family leave laws, so be sure to check with your human resource manager to determine if you are entitled to additional state leave. The states that currently have state family leave acts are:

- California
- Connecticut
- District of Columbia
- Hawaii
- Maine
- Minnesota
- New Jersey
- Oregon
- Rhode Island
- Vermont
- Washington
- Wisconsin

Additionally, California has a state disability law that says that parents of newborns, as well as parents of newly adopted children of any age, qualify for a disability leave that provides the new parents with a percentage of their pay, as well as job security. You may also qualify for paid maternity or paternity leave or special adoption leave under your company's policies.

Insurance and Planning for the Future

Once the child is placed with you, you can contact your health insurance company about adding the child to your policy. You will need to have family coverage to add your child. If you do not have family coverage, you may need to wait until the next enrollment period (which usually occurs four times per year) to change your coverage to family coverage. If you have family coverage already, contact your insurer before the adoption is finalized and ask what you need to do to have the child added. You want to be sure your child is covered from the moment of the adoption forward, so this means starting the paperwork before the adoption is completed.

> ### Adoption Answer
> Many states now have their adoption forms online. Check your state court system's website for your state's forms. For example, you can see New York's forms at:
>
> **www.courts.state.ny.us/ forms/familycourt/ adoption.shtml**

Life Insurance

If you do not already have *life insurance*, it is a good idea to consider purchasing some. If you are married, you will probably want to name your spouse as beneficiary. If you are unmarried, you will want to name your child as beneficiary. Some parents also like to purchase life insurance for their new child, but it is often a better idea to create an investment account for the child.

You may also wish to consider creating a 529 College Savings Account for your child to help defray the expenses of a college education. There are many options and it is important to create a complete financial plan for your family. Talk to your financial planner.

> **Adoption Answer**
> If your company does not currently offer an adoption assistance program, information about starting one is available through:
>
> **The Adoption-Friendly Workplace Program**
> 877-777-4222
> **www.adoption friendlyworkplace.org**

Wills

You will also want to have a will drawn up. Once you adopt a child, he or she inherits from you through the laws of your state, so a will is not important for that reason. It is important because in your will you can name a guardian who would

> **Adoption Answer**
> Read your state's adoption laws at:
>
> **www.law.cornell.edu/ wex**

have custody of your child should you die (and if your spouse or partner should also die). When choosing a guardian, be sure to choose someone who has similar beliefs as yours and who will be close to your child. Be sure to talk this decision over with the potential guardian. If the guardian you name is unable or unwilling to take on the responsibility of guardianship, the court will find a replacement among your family members, but you want to have a hand in this decision. Name an alternate guardian in case something happens to your first choice.

Chapter 4

SECOND-PARENT ADOPTION

Second-parent adoptions are often referred to as *stepparent adoptions*. The child lives with one legal parent and the child's other parent may be deceased, completely out of touch, or without custody. This legal parent remarries and the stepparent, at some point, wishes to adopt the child. These adoptions are quite common and are generally simpler than other kinds of adoptions. If a stepparent does not adopt the child, he or she might have an important parental role in the child's life, but in the eyes of the law, he or she has no authority over or legal connection to the child. The child cannot inherit from the stepparent (unless the stepparent specifically leaves something to him or her in a will) or receive any survivor benefits from the stepparent. The stepparent cannot make medical decisions or educational decisions for the child (unless specifically authorized by the parent) and if the stepparent and the legal parent divorce or break up, the stepparent has no legal right to spend time with the child or seek custody or visitation. Additionally, if the legal parent dies, the stepparent would not automatically be named as the child's guardian or be given custody.

Very often a stepparent is already an *emotional parent* to the child—someone who fills the role of a parent in the child's life and the child is deeply attached to. A stepparent or second-parent adoption legalizes the role the stepparent already has in the child's life.

Deciding to Adopt a Stepchild

The decision to adopt a stepchild should not be made lightly. Once you adopt your stepchild, he or she is your child and the adoption cannot be undone (although in some states there is a short window in which consent to the adoption can be withdrawn). You will be financially and legally responsible for the child, and should you get divorced, you could be liable for child support. A stepchild who is adopted becomes your legal child in all ways.

A stepchild who you adopt is able to inherit from you. If you have other children, this adopted stepchild will be treated exactly the same as your other children when it comes to inheritance. Sometimes this can cause bad feelings in families. If you want your adopted stepchild to be treated differently, it is important that you have a will made specifying what you want to leave to each child.

If the child's other parent is deceased, the adoption might be an emotional issue for the child. Some children are resistant to the idea of a stepparent replacing the deceased parent and want to reserve a special role for that parent. In this kind of situation, it is a good idea to explore the child's feelings and possibly seek some family counseling to help sort it out. It may take some time for the child to be ready to take this step. Some stepparents never adopt their stepchildren and there is nothing wrong with that choice either. It is important for everyone involved in the decision to realize that an adoption does not in any way insult or denigrate the role the deceased parent played in the child's life or the importance he or she still has for the child. A stepparent adoption is something that changes the future, not the past.

Another major stumbling block in second-parent adoptions is the way the legal parent and the stepparent feel. Some stepparents are hesitant to take on a legal role in the child's life. Particularly if they do not have biological children of their own, some stepparents feel unsure about the responsibilities of parenthood. It can also be daunting to feel as if you are taking over for a parent who is deceased or out of the picture.

In other situations, the marriage might be experiencing some trouble and the parent and stepparent might see the adoption as providing some additional glue to help hold it together. It is important to understand that a stepparent adoption is not a quick fix for marital problems. Doing an adoption at this stage in your life will only make it more difficult should you divorce, and will prove even more damaging for the child.

A newly married couple might feel as if they need to hurry to do a stepparent adoption in order to make their new family complete. However, it may simply be too soon in the relationship for the adoption to feel right for the child and everyone else involved. It takes time for a new stepparent to really become a parent in the child's eyes. This relationship is one that needs to develop on its own, and at its own pace. You cannot force a child to think of a stepparent as a parent, but it is something that happens as their relationship grows.

If you have other children and you are adopting your stepchild, you need to consider the feelings of your children. Some children feel that the adopted child will somehow usurp their positions. It is similar to the way a child feels when a sibling is born into the family, but is more intense because your children clearly know that this new child is not related to you or the rest of the family in quite the same way. Taking some time to help your existing children accept the adoption will help everyone adjust. It is a good idea to have open and frank discussions with everyone in the family about the adoption. Family counseling can help you work through many problems.

If you adopt a stepchild, your parents become your adopted child's grandparents. This can go smoothly or cause some problems. If you have been married to the child's parent for a long time, the child has probably already established a relationship with your parents. If this is a relatively new situation, it may take some time. Regardless of how things have been up to this point, it is important that your parents understand that this child is now fully and completely yours, and by extension, theirs. They should work hard to make sure they treat all of their grandchildren equally or there is sure to be resentment. It is important that second-parent adoptions are done for the right reason—to solidify a relationship that has already been established between the stepparent and the child and to provide legal rights to the child and stepparent.

Qualifications to Adopt

If you are married to the child's legal parent, you can seek a second-parent adoption. In some states you do not have to be married, but can simply be partners. (See Chapter 9 for information about same-sex couples.) It is usually best to wait until you have been married at least one year before seeking to adopt your stepchild. This demonstrates to the court that you have had time to establish a close relationship with the child and that your marriage is stable (some states require this).

Notice or Consent

The parent who has custody of the child must consent to the adoption and in some states must actually readopt the child as well (so that you are adopting the child together as a couple). While this seems silly, it is simply a formality and does nothing to change the relationship between the child and the existing parent.

If your stepchild has another legal or biological parent who is alive, then that parent is entitled to some kind of notice of the adoption and the chance to deny consent. This other parent must consent to give up all rights to the child or fail to respond to the legal notice that is given in order for the adoption to occur. This legal notice is done by giving the parent papers explaining the intention to adopt the child. In some states these documents can be mailed to the parent or personally *served* (given to him or her in person by a process server). If the other parent cannot be located, you may need to go through a process in which the notice is published in a newspaper. It is crucial that notice be given correctly because if you do not exactly follow your state's requirements, that parent could come back later and attempt to undo the adoption.

Stepparent adoption is also possible when the parent has had his or her parental rights terminated by the court (such as in an abuse or neglect situation). In some states, if the other parent does not give consent, his or her rights can be terminated in certain circumstances, such as if he or she has not had any contact with the child for a long period of time. If you give the biological parent notice and he or she does not consent, the only way to get around it is to prove neglect and have his or her parental rights terminated or to show the parent has abandoned the child. There is no way to force a biological parent to agree to an adoption, even if the adoption would clearly be in the best interest of the child. Also, a court cannot decide to let the adoption go forward if the other parent is opposed to it. If you are in a situation where the biological parent will not consent and you cannot find a way to terminate rights, remember that being a parent is really a state of mind. You can think of yourself as the child's parent and act like his or her parent, even if the law will not recognize you as such. Some families that have confronted this problem act as if the stepparent is really a parent. Once the child is an adult, you can legally adopt him or her then to make it official. What makes a parent is what one does, not what a piece of paper says.

If you cannot adopt, there are some things you and your spouse or partner can do to safeguard your relationship with the child. Your spouse or partner can include a provision in his or her will naming you as guardian. He or she can identify you to the child's school as a person who has permission to pick up the child, and attend school events and parent-teacher conferences. Your spouse or partner can also complete a form allowing you to make medical decisions for the child.

Pre-Adoption Procedures

Some states waive the requirement of a home study in second-parent adoptions; some states have laws that require it, but permit judges to waive it; and, other states require stepparents (and the child's existing parent if he or she must also adopt the child) to go through the home study and background check process. Usually when a home study is required, the primary focus will be on the stepparent, his or her history, how long they have been married, and what kind of relationship he or she has with the child. However, when it is required, the home study process is usually minimal. The state department of social services usually performs the home study when it is required.

The states that do not require home studies for second-parent adoptions include:

- Alabama
- Alaska
- Arizona
- California
- Colorado
- Connecticut
- Florida
- Georgia
- Maryland
- Michigan
- Minnesota
- Mississippi
- Nebraska
- Ohio
- Pennsylvania
- South Carolina
- Texas

The states where home studies can be waived for second-parent adoptions include:

- Arizona
- District of Columbia
- Missouri
- Nevada
- New Hampshire
- Oklahoma
- Oregon
- Utah

Second-Parent Adoption Process

Stepparent adoptions can be handled on your own without an attorney more easily than other types of adoption, although it is a good idea to hire an attorney to ensure that the case is handled properly, particularly if you have to give notice to the child's other legal parent. Some states require representation by an attorney.

If you do choose to handle the adoption on your own, you need to contact the court in your state that does adoptions to obtain forms and get information about the filing procedures.

A second-parent adoption follows the same procedure as any other adoption, with the only difference being the home study is sometimes not required. (See Chapter 3 for more details on adoption procedures.) In many states, when a second parent adopts the child, the biological parent that he or she is married to must also adopt the child, so that both people must complete the paperwork. This does nothing to change the biological parent's status and is simply an antiquated procedure. It used to be that only married couples could adopt a child. Some states still require that the second-parent adoption be done by both parents so that both names go through the entire process and both names end up on the birth certificate at the end of the process.

Chapter 5

DOMESTIC AGENCY ADOPTION

Most people who adopt use an agency to help them locate a birth mother or a child, and to help process the adoption. If you are adopting a child born in the United States, the agency you use will be a *domestic agency* (meaning it is located in the United States and is processing the adoption of a U.S. citizen). Domestic agencies are not all alike. The first important distinction is between public and private agencies.

A *public agency* refers to a state department of social services or department of family and children's services. These agencies handle the adoption of children who were in foster care and have been freed for adoption by the state's courts or who have been surrendered by their birth parents. Most of these children are not babies and many are special needs children. There are many children available for adoption through these state agencies.

Private agencies are those run by private entities. Some are nonprofit, while others are for-profit businesses. Some are run by religious organizations, while others are nonsectarian. You will find that there is a wide selection of private agencies to choose from.

Public Agencies

Public agency adoptions have the same requirements as other types of adoptions, including the home study, background check, and court procedure to finalize the adoption. Public agency adoptions are usually the fastest and least expensive type of adoption. However, since the children tend to be older, the transition and adjustment period is often more difficult. All children who are available for adoption in a state are shown in the state's photolisting book. The books show a photo and description of each child.

Foster Care

The *foster care* system is set up to provide homes for children who have been removed from their homes because of abuse, neglect, and occasionally juvenile delinquency. Children who have been abandoned or voluntarily placed with the state by their parents are also placed in foster care. These children are placed in the temporary care of the state while their parents deal with the court system or the court determines that their parents abandoned them. Many times these children are returned to their parents if the court decides that no abuse or neglect occurred or if the parents meet the requirements set up by the agency (such as counseling, rehab, child care classes, maintaining a stable lifestyle, and so on) and the parents are deemed fit to care for the children.

In other instances, the children are never reunited with their parents. Most states now make an effort to move the case through the court system quickly so that the children are either returned home or are freed for adoption and do not languish in foster care for years. The federal *Adoption and Safe Families Act* states that if a child has been in foster care for at least fifteen months or if his or her parents abandoned the child, the parental rights can be terminated and the child can be freed for adoption. For the children who do not return home, the court severs the biological parents' ties to the children and frees them for adoption.

Many adoptions occur by the foster parents who care for the children while their case is pending or while their parents are trying to meet the agency's requirements for return. Becoming a foster parent is one route to public agency adoption. To become a foster parent, you must first identify the private agencies that contract for foster care with the state. In most states, the public agency itself does not directly handle foster care placement. Prospective foster care parents must work with a private agency that handles the state agency's contract for foster care.

To become a foster parent, you must:

- complete a series of classes;
- provide financial, personal, and health information about yourself and your family;
- be able to provide appropriate housing for a child or children;
- be prepared for ongoing contact with caseworkers; and,
- understand that a foster care parent's job is to care for the child, while helping to reunite him or her with the biological parents. (Adoption is not an option until the child has been freed for adoption.)

When you become a foster parent, you will make yourself available to children who may or may not be freed for adoption. At the time of initial placement, you have no way of knowing how the case will ultimately be resolved. As a foster parent, you will receive a small monthly stipend that is meant to cover the child's expenses and you will also have to follow the caseworker's instructions. While you are the foster care parent, the child is in the custody of the state and the caseworker will have absolute authority over major decisions involving the child. Foster parents have very little rights when it comes to the children they care for. Contact your local public agency for information about which private agencies handle foster care and how you can apply.

Adoption Answer

Find contacts for foster care agencies in your state at:

www.fosterparenting.com

Get support and information about foster care adoption at:

www.DaveThomas Foundationfor Adoption.org

Legal Risk Placement

Legal risk placement occurs when you accept a child who you would like to adopt but has not yet been completely freed for adoption. The intent of the placement is for the child to begin to develop a relationship with you and to begin to put down roots. However, the child is not legally free for adoption yet and something may happen that could prevent the adoption from happening. While you are waiting for the child to be freed for adoption, you are acting as a foster care parent, since the state has custody and control of the child. This kind of placement allows you to get a jump on the whole process by bonding with your child before the finalization, but you must accept the risk that the adoption may not be finalized.

Traditional Adoption

Another method of adopting a child through a public agency is the traditional method, in which the child is not placed until the adoption is complete. The child remains in foster care until the legal process is finalized and then comes home to the adoptive parents. This is the least risky of all the public agency adoption choices, but it can also be the most emotionally difficult for a child old enough to understand what is happening. There is no transition period as there is in foster care placement or legal risk placement.

Public Agency Adoption Issues

When adopting a child through a public agency, make sure to obtain full medical records and family histories if available. Before you agree to the adoption, you want to get as much information as you can. The child may have a history or background that does not work for you. (It is important to be honest and face the fact that not every child is the right child for you.) The caseworkers who manage the child while he or she is in foster care have access to the biological parents and can obtain this information. They can also provide information about assessments and evaluations that have been done while the child has been in foster care.

> **Adoption Answer**
>
> Find your state public adoption agency online at:
>
> **www.childwelfare.gov/ nad/index.cfm**

Because the child is usually leaving parents that are alive and have some kind of relationship with the child (no matter how dysfunctional), there are significant transition issues for the child and the adoptive parent. If the child is old enough, he or she will remember his or her biological parents and will have some kind of attachment to them, even if they were terrible parents. It takes a lot of time and patience to help children adjust. It also takes time for them to learn to trust adoptive parents. Many of these children were abused, malnourished, or emotionally damaged.

Moving into a loving, nurturing home can be a shock. Some adoptive parents report that their new children raid the refrigerator and gorge, or hide food in their rooms—certain that soon they would starve again. Other children have been known to steal from new family members or harm new siblings.

There are numerous behavioral issues you might face after the adoption. A good counselor or therapist is essential to help everyone make a smooth adjustment. Your social worker from the agency can provide some help with adjustment or can recommend a private counselor. It is also a good idea to get involved with an adoption support group.

Special Needs

Many public agency adoptive children have special needs. Special needs children are those that take longer to place and include:

- school-age children or teens;
- children with physical, mental, or emotional disabilities;
- sibling groups that must stay together; and,
- children of certain racial or ethnic groups that are difficult to place.

Simply because a child is described as special needs does not mean that there is anything wrong with him or her. It just means that this child is difficult to place. Your home might be the perfect place for a special needs child. For this reason, it is important to find out what evaluations have been done, what the specialists recommend, and what kind of care or treatment the child needs.

> **Adoption Answer**
>
> Get tips on helping an older child deal with adoption at:
>
> **www.familyhelper.net/ arc/old.html**

Learn about the child's exposure to or use of drugs or alcohol, and have a treatment plan in place to deal with these issues. Get detailed information about the child's behavior and where he or she has lived and who has cared for him or her in the past. Ask for copies of all reports, evaluations, and assessments. Special needs children may appeal to people who do not wish to care for a baby or toddler, or who have special skills dealing with disabled children or in working with teens. Additionally, special needs children are sometimes easier to adopt because the agency is willing to overlook certain problems with the adoptive family in order to help the children find a home.

Adopting a special needs child can be a challenge, but it can also be tremendously rewarding. Special needs kids often recognize the fact that they are hard to place. Sometimes the adjustment process can be difficult because they tend to erect barriers since they have had their hopes dashed so many times in the past. Adopting a special needs child does not work for everyone, but many families find it to be rewarding.

Financial Assistance for Public Agency Adoptions

Because of the difficult nature of many public agency adoptions and because many of the children adopted do have special needs, there is special funding available to assist the parents in caring for the child after the adoption.

> ### Adoption Answer
>
> The National Child Resource Center for Adoption can provide information and support for those adopting special needs children. Contact them at:
>
> **National Child Resource Center for Adoption**
> 16250 Northland Drive
> Suite 120
> Southfield, MI 48075
> 248-443-0306
> **www.nrcadoption.org**
>
> Other sites that can provide information include:
>
> **http://special-needs. adoption.com**
>
> and
>
> **www.spaulding.org**

Title IV-E Assistance

Special needs children may qualify for federal funding assistance. The child may be receiving Social Security Insurance (SSI) payments already, but may also qualify for Adoption and Safe Families Act (ASFA) funding. ASFA provides financial assistance for children who are adopted and:

- were receiving *Temporary Assistance to Needy Families* (TANF) (in other words, welfare) in the birth home or
- were eligible for SSI in the birth home, which means they were disabled and were in a home that met certain financial requirements.

When you are negotiating your adoption with your public agency, you need to ask about eligibility for this funding. You can apply directly through your local social services or family services department. Usually the social worker who handles your adoption will help you apply.

Adoption Assistance Agreement

An *adoption assistance agreement* is a contract between the adoptive parents and the state agency, describing the ongoing monthly payments the state will make to the parents after the adoption is complete to help with the expense of raising the child. The payments are often for a few hundred dollars per month.

> **Adoption Answer**
>
> For more information about state subsidies, visit:
>
> **www.adopting.org/ subsidy.html**

The agreement is made before the adoption takes place and is in effect as long as the child is a minor. The agreement may also include provisions for assistance with the child's medical expenses (see the Medicaid section later in this chapter). Some states include additional funding amounts for children that are especially difficult to care for. These are known as *level of care* (LOC) payments.

These agreements are common for special needs adoptions where the child is known to need continuing care or services that are outside of the normal medical needs children experience. They are provided so that families will adopt these children and not have to worry about

> ## Adoption Answer
> For information on what your state pays for adoption assistance, see:
>
> **www.nacac.org/ subsidy_stateprofiles.html**

affording the care the child will need (and it is still less expensive than paying to keep a child in foster care). The agreement is enforceable. If there is future disagreement about it, an administrative hearing is held to resolve the problem. Do not finalize your adoption until this document is signed.

If you negotiate an agreement, make sure it:

- is in writing;
- contains beginning and ending dates for the payments;
- specifies the amount of payments and any changes to the amount as the child ages;
- does not put excessive restrictions or requirements on you after the adoption occurs;
- specifies the reporting or certification you need to comply with to continue to receive payments;
- lists all services to be provided by the state;
- explains how subsidies or services can be increased or decreased and what kind of notice is required;
- describes Medicaid coverage for the child;
- explains what happens if you move out of state or if both adoptive parents die;
- describes what you need to do to get an administrative hearing should you need one; and,
- takes into account your child's needs and your family's situation.

Medicaid

A special needs child may qualify for Medicaid. The state Medicaid program will pay many of his or her medical expenses both before and after the adoption. If you have a family health care policy, your child can also receive treatment under that plan—it may cover some of the things that Medicaid does not. Medicaid is a federal program, but is administered by each state individually with different rights and procedures in each state. Your social worker will provide information about your child's Medicaid eligibility.

> **Adoption Answer**
>
> For more information about Medicaid, visit:
>
> **www.cms.hhs.gov/ medicaid**

Tax Credits

Parents adopting a special needs child are entitled to a $10,630 tax credit, without having to show any expenses. This applies to families earning under $150,000 per year. Those earning between $150,000 and $189,999 receive a reduced credit in proportion to income. This is a credit that is nonrefundable—meaning that you cannot get money refunded above your tax liability. But if you do have a lower income, you can claim the credit over a five-year period so that you can use more of it. There are also some state tax credits available. Check with your tax preparer to find out what your state provides. (See Chapter 3 for more information about tax credits.)

> **Adoption Answer**
>
> IRS Publication 968 explains tax credits in greater detail. Find it at:
>
> **www.irs.gov**

For the purposes of the tax credit, a special needs child is one who cannot be placed with adoptive parents without providing a subsidy.

A reasonable but unsuccessful effort must be made to place the child for adoption without a subsidy, unless it is in the child's best interests to remain with prospective adoptive parents with whom they have significant emotional ties. Factors or conditions related to the special needs determination may include ethnic background, age, membership in a minority or sibling group, the presence of a medical condition, or physical, mental, or emotional disabilities.

Other Assistance

Organizations for parents of special needs children (including those referenced earlier in this chapter) will provide support and assistance as you adopt and raise a special needs child. If your child is of school age, or will soon be of school age, you will need to begin to learn your way around the special education process.

Adoption Answer

For information and resources about special education, visit:

www.seriweb.com

The federal Department of Education has a section about special education located at:

www.ed.gov/about/ offices/list/osers/osep/ index.html

Wrights Law is an excellent site devoted to helping parents navigate the system. Find it at:

www.wrightslaw.com

The National Dissemination Center for Children with Disabilities is another excellent resource. Find it at:

www.nichcy.org

Biological Relatives

Another important issue is the child's *biological relatives*. While a court can sever legal ties between a child and his or her biological family, the court cannot change the emotional ties that exist when an older child is adopted. For this reason, some courts permit adoptive parents and biological relatives of the child to create and record *kinship agreements*. These agreements set out a plan for how the child will continue to have contact with important family members (such as grandparents, siblings, aunts, and uncles). This prevents a child from feeling totally cut off from his or her family and ethnic heritage. (See Chapter 10 for more information about kinship agreements.)

Agency Liability

All agencies have a duty to fully disclose information about the child being placed for adoption. This duty is particularly important when working with a public agency, since most children placed through it have had difficult home lives or suffer disabilities. The agency must disclose to you:

- how and why the child came into the state's care;
- why the child remained in the care of the state;
- why the parental rights were terminated; and,
- why the agency decided to place the child.

> **Adoption Answer**
>
> Some states provide special tuition assistance or waivers for foster care children who have been adopted. For information, see:
>
> **www.nacac.org/ subsidyfactsheets/ tuition.html**

It is also important that the caseworker explain to you the causal relationship that exists between a child's home life and his or her behavior—how the things he or she went through have caused him or her to act the way he or she does and how it might affect future behavior. The caseworker is responsible for reading the entire file and disclosing all the information in it to you. Failure to do so is negligence on the part of the agency. There is some dispute about how far a worker must go. Some states say that a caseworker should make reasonable efforts to investigate the background of the family the child came from, while most states say that the agency is not required to take investigative steps.

The child's file should include the following:

- hospital records;
- records from doctors' offices;
- the child's HIV history (including testing);
- school records; and,
- what family background is known.

An agency that fails to disclose all of this information can be sued for *wrongful adoption*. Some agencies in the past have placed a child and lied about his or her history or purposefully failed to disclose important information. When a court finds that wrongful adoption has occurred, money damages are awarded. These damages can be *punitive* (to punish the agency) and can also be *compensatory*, to pay back the family for the medical or psychological care it has had to pay that it did not anticipate. Sometimes damages are also awarded to pay the family back for physical harm caused by the adoptive child (if, for example, the child has caused damage to property or harmed family members). The family cannot recover the ordinary costs of raising a child. In a few rare cases, the family has been allowed to dissolve the adoption and return the child to the agency.

> ### Adoption Answer
> The Child Welfare League of America publishes standards that public adoption agencies should try to follow. Find more information at:
>
> **www.cwla.org**

The best way to avoid these kinds of problems is to insist on complete disclosure, to go over documents carefully, and to use an adoption attorney who will help you make sure your rights are protected.

Private Agency Adoption

Private agencies have infants as well as older children to place for adoption. An infant will take the longest to adopt (because you may need to wait for one to be born), while older children are placed more quickly. Most parents using private agencies are looking for babies.

Evaluating a Private Agency

The first step to working with a private agency is to carefully select one. Since you will pay an application fee, it is usually not a good idea to apply to more than one agency at a time. Be sure to evaluate agencies carefully. (See Chapter 2 for more information about this.)

Once you have narrowed down your search to a few agencies, talk to the adoption specialist at your state department of social services. He or she can tell you what the agencies are like and what kind of information the state has available about them. Check with the Better Business Bureau in your state to determine if any complaints have been filed against the agency. Talk with other adoptive parents and find out what they have heard about the agency. Ask for referrals and talk to other adoptive parents who have used the agency.

Fees

Compare the home study costs and other fees that each agency charges. Less might not always be better if you feel a more expensive agency does a better job. Be absolutely certain that the agency and the social worker who does the home study are licensed in your state. Most states do not set limits on the fees an agency may charge, but do require that they must not exceed what is considered *reasonable and customary*. Cost can range anywhere from $4,000 to $30,000, depending on the agency. Agencies run by religious groups tend to cost less. Some agencies charge a flat fee, while others charge for each service separately. Be sure to get a complete list of what is covered by a flat fee.

The following are fees typically charged and the average cost of each. Your costs may be higher or lower, but this list gives a rough estimate of what to expect to pay in fees. The average costs include:

- application — $250;
- home study — $1,200;
- post placement services — $500;
- psychological evaluations of parents — $200 each;
- physical exams for parents — $75 each;
- document fees — varies (often $1,000);
- court fees and legal costs — varies by state (up to $12,000);
- advertising fees — $2,000;
- birth mother living costs — varies;
- medical expenses for mother and baby — varies;
- legal fees for birth mother — may be $1,000; and,
- counseling — $1,000.

Adoption Answer

To find a list of private agencies in your area to search for licensed adoption agencies in your state, visit the Children's Bureau Adoption website at:

www.adoptuskids.org

Be sure to compare fees between several agencies so that you have an understanding of what the average fees are like in your area. You may be asked to pay for most expenses up front or you may be able to pay for them as they occur. Find out how the agency requires you to pay before applying.

Expenses

Be skeptical if the agency takes money paid for your birth mother's expenses and places it in an *escrow pool* out of which it pays all birth mothers' individual expenses for placing babies with the agency. With this method, you do not pay your birth mother's actual expenses, but instead pay an average cost that takes into account high expenses some birth mothers have. Most states require an accounting be made to the court, listing the expenses the adoptive parents have paid for. Because most of the babies available for placement have not been born yet, there is the very real chance that the birth mother will change her mind before placement occurs. Always find out what the agency's policy is about the fees you have already paid — can you roll them over to use for another birth mother should the birth mother you choose change her mind? Idaho is the only state that requires birth parents to reimburse adoptive parents if the birth parents change their minds and decide not to place the child for adoption.

Some states permit adoptive parents to pay for the birth mother's living expenses during her pregnancy. Adoptive parents pay for the medical expenses of both birth mother and baby. The baby will not be covered by your health insurance plan until the child is placed with you, so these expenses are out-of-pocket expenses for adoptive parents, unless the birth mother has health insurance coverage (or the adoptive parents purchase a policy for her).

Many adoptive parents feel a need to give the birth mother a gift after the birth. While this may seem like a wonderful gesture, it in fact can cause problems for you since many states prohibit any compensation to the birth mother for the adoption. This is intended to prevent the buying and selling of babies, but also prevents extravagant gifts. Small tokens of appreciation may be acceptable, but you need to check with your agency and your attorney before doing anything. (See Chapter 7 for more information about the length of time living expenses can be paid.)

Interstate Issues

Depending on what state you live in, you may find that there are not many children available to adopt from within your state. If this is the case, you may need to adopt a child who is born in another state. To do so, you and the agency must be in compliance with the *Interstate Compact,* a federal law that governs how children are transported between states for adoption purposes. Each state has an Interstate Compact administrator. The administrators in the state you live in and the state you are adopting from must both agree to the adoption. Your adoption agency and attorney will handle this technicality for you.

Ethnic Concerns

You also need to be aware of a federal law called the *Multiethnic Placement Act.* It denies federal funding to adoption agencies that delay or deny placement because of race (in other words, wait to place a child only with parents of the same race as the child). If you are interested in adopting a child with an ethnic background that is different from yours, ask if the agency complies with this statute. If you believe you have been denied a placement due to race, talk to your adoption attorney or contact your state attorney general.

> ### Adoption Answer
> For support in raising a multi-ethnic family, contact the Association of Multiethnic Americans at:
>
> **www.ameasite.org**

Dealing with Problems

While hopefully your adoption will go smoothly, sometimes problems crop up. Not all problems are deal-breakers, so don't jump to conclusions should something come up in your adoption.

The best way to avert problems is to work with an experienced adoption attorney who has handled many adoptions and whom you trust. He or she will shepherd you through the process. Working with a well-established and respected adoption agency is also key.

Should a problem happen, first try to resolve it yourself, through calls to the caseworker or adoption agency. Often there are just simply communication problems that can be easily resolved. If you need certain documents and are not getting them, a written request may move things along. It may also help to speak to your caseworker's supervisor if you continue to hit a brick wall. If you are unable to make any headway, contact your attorney.

Public Agency Adoption Warning Signs

- The caseworker does not provide details about the child's background
- You are not encouraged to get to know the child well before the adoption
- The child's foster parents are not supportive or helpful of your adoption
- There are things about the child that make you wonder or that bother you, which are not addressed by the caseworker
- You are not given the opportunity to see the child's medical records

Private Agency Adoption Warning Signs

- The agency does not return your calls
- The agency requests a large upfront fee with no breakdown indicated
- The agency is unwilling to provide references
- You are not told the number of adoptions placed each year
- The agency is unwilling to explain how it finds birth mothers
- You feel pressured to sign the agency agreement
- Open adoption is not an option
- You are guaranteed a child sooner if you pay more

Chapter 6

INTERNATIONAL ADOPTION

International adoption is the adoption of a child from a country outside the United States. International adoption has become more popular in recent years with publicity about how many waiting children there are in countries around the world. International adoption is an excellent choice if you do not want to wait to find a birth mother or newborn baby and do not mind adopting a child who is not a newborn. The procedure is not as complicated as some people expect it to be and the costs end up being about the same when you factor in travel expenses. The procedure is similar to those for domestic adoptions but involves extra steps such as dealing with the U.S. Department of Homeland Security's Citizenship and Immigration Services (USCIS) — once known as the Immigration and Naturalization Service (INS) — and U.S. and overseas courts.

Choosing an Agency

You should always work with an agency to do an international adoption, since it is extremely difficult to evaluate and choose an overseas adoption facilitator. Some private agencies handle only domestic adoption or only international adoption, while others handle both types. To find an agency, check with your local agencies, talk to members of your adoption support group, or join a group specifically for international adoptive families to find out which agency parents used.

Adoption Answer

The Joint Council of International Children's Services has a list of agencies it accredits that can be found at:

www.jcics.org

The International Adoption Consortium also has a similar list that can be found at:

www.welcomegarden.com /agencies.html

For more information on choosing an international adoption agency, see:

www.adopting.org/ choosagn.html

Adoption Answer

You can search for agencies by the country you wish to adopt from or by the state you live in at:

http://directory. adoption.com

Choosing a Country

At the time this book was written, the top ten countries from which U.S. adoptions took place were:

- China
- Colombia
- Ethiopia
- Guatemala
- India
- Kazakhstan
- Philippines
- Russia
- South Korea
- Ukraine

Each country has its own requirements. Most countries require that a couple be married for at least three years and have age limits. Russia requires that parents make two trips to the country—one to identify the child and the second to adopt him or her. South Korea does not allow adoptions by parents who are more than 30% overweight. You need to carefully research the requirements of the countries you are interested in before making a decision.

Some parents go into the adoption process knowing which country they want to adopt from, while others have no preference and choose a country that seems to fit them best. When choosing a country, you will want to consider:

- your feelings about each country's culture and history;
- your feelings about the physical attributes common to children from that country;
- the type of care children placed for adoption receive in the country you are considering;
- your own background and family history;
- your feeling about raising children of an ethnicity different from yours;
- the type of medical care birth mothers receive in each country;
- whether or not you need to travel to that country to adopt;
- the length of stay required and the number of visits required to adopt in each country;
- the ease with which paperwork is processed in that country; and,
- the experiences of other adoptive parents who have adopted from that country.

> ### Adoption Answer
> The U.S. Department of State has country-specific information available on its website. The document for each country on the site spells out the requirements and U.S. agencies that handle adoptions for that country. Visit it at:
>
> **http://travel.state.gov/ family/adoption/country/ country_369.html**

The selection of a country is a matter of personal choice. There is not room in this book to discuss the differences between the various countries, so it is important that you do some research on your own. Start with the U.S. Department of State website and the websites about adoption in the various countries listed in Appendix A.

Choosing a Child

In some countries, you go to the orphanage and actually select a child that appeals to you, while other countries assign a child to you. If you adopt from South Korea, you will not meet your child until he or she is delivered to you at the airport in the United States, although you will receive a photograph in advance. Medical concerns are important to consider when selecting a child. Because the standard of health care varies greatly overseas, many children available for placement are developmentally delayed or suffer from a minor or major health problem. Before you choose a child, obtain photos, videotape if possible, as well as whatever medical records can be translated into English. Have them reviewed by a pediatrician who specializes in evaluating children for overseas adoptions. If you will not have access to these documents before you travel overseas, make arrangements before you leave to fax or send these items to the doctor while you are there. This kind of doctor can evaluate the child from the records and make an educated inference about what kinds of problems the child is or may be experiencing. Based on the evaluation, you may decide to adopt a different child.

> **Adoption Answer**
>
> The American Academy of Pediatrics provides a list of pediatricians specializing in adoption. View the list at:
>
> **www.aap.org/sections/ adoption/adopt-states/ adoption-map.htm**

It is imperative that the child you select is legally released for adoption by the country of origin. Only children who are completely released for adoption will be eligible for adoption in the eyes of the U.S. government. You will need your agency's help to obtain this release.

You have the right to turn down the child that is offered to you. Often this happens after the medical reports are examined or after you meet the child. Some parents do not wish to adopt a child with serious medical problems, while others are comfortable doing so. This is a matter of personal choice. It is important that you work with professionals you can trust who can give you good advice about medical history and developmental delays.

If you decide not to accept the child, you do not return to square one. All of the paperwork you have provided will still be valid, but you will have to wait for another child to be selected for you. The process differs in each country. You may have to return home (if you are visiting the country) or you may be able to have another child assigned to you while you are there. Be sure to ask your agency how this process will work when you begin the process so there are no surprises.

Dealing with Paperwork

Your application for the adoption will be made to your local agency. They will be your primary contact throughout the entire adoption process and will handle most of the contact with the overseas agency. The application and home study process for an international adoption is similar to that required for a domestic adoption, with a few extra steps. All of these documents must be translated and then approved by the agency in the country you are adopting from (your agency will arrange for the translation). Additionally, many of the documents you provide must be authenticated, meaning they must bear a raised seal from the agency or office issuing them (there is an additional fee for obtaining authenticated copies). You may need to include photos of your home for review by the overseas agency. In addition to the usual home study and application, you will also need to obtain preliminary USCIS approval. If you are married, one spouse must be a U.S. citizen and your combined income must be 25% above the poverty level. You are not eligible if you have been convicted of a felony or certain misdemeanors.

The Process

Because each country has its own requirements, there is no one set procedure for international adoptions. However, the procedure you must follow in the United States is the same.

You will need to complete the application, home study process (your home study will be used both by the agency as well as the USCIS to determine that you are qualified to adopt), and background check (which is also submitted to USCIS). Fingerprints must be completed at a USCIS office using the provided Form FD-258. Fingerprinting will occur at your home USCIS office if you are in the United States, or at an embassy or consulate if you are abroad.

Before you even have a child selected for adoption, you can begin the adoption process by filing Form I-600A, *Petition to Classify Orphan as an Immediate Relative*. It begins the process of classifying the child you will adopt as an *immediate relative*. The fee for filing is $545. You also need to file Form I-864, *Affidavit of Support*. It is an affidavit about your ability to support a child. All USCIS forms must be filed at your local office. (See Appendix C for a copy of these forms.)

Once you have been approved to adopt by the agency and the U.S. government, you will need to learn about the requirements for finalizing the adoption in the overseas country your child is from. This may include a court appearance in the country's court. If so, it is important that you have a translator along, which your agency can help you arrange. You may need to travel to the country and stay there for a period of time before you are permitted to adopt. You may need to appear in court in the country to finalize the adoption. Obtain several official copies of any documents you are provided by the officials you work with in the country.

Dealing with Immigration

To bring your child to the United States, you must do the following.

- Use Form I-600 to petition to have the identified child classified as an *immediate relative*. (If you filed Form I-600A, there is no fee for Form I-600. If you did not, there is a $545 fee).
- Apply for the child to immigrate to the United States.

You must physically see your child in person before you are permitted to adopt him or her. If a married couple is adopting, only one member of the couple must see the child in order for the adoption to be valid. If you are not adopting your child abroad and instead are only adopting him or her in the United States, be sure you check the appropriate box on the *Petition to Classify Orphan as an Immediate Relative*.

> **Adoption Answer**
> You can complete the forms online at:
>
> **www.uscis.gov**

Visas

A *visa* is a document that gives tentative permission for the child to enter the United States from a foreign country. The visa itself does not have complete authority, since immigration officials have the final say upon the child's entrance to the country.

To apply for a visa for your child, use Form IR-3, for children adopted in a foreign country, or Form IR-4, for children who will be adopted in the United States. The application must be submitted to the U.S. embassy or consular office in the country the child is being adopted from. The child must be seen by the consular or embassy official and must also be examined by a physician approved by the consulate or embassy. Certain contagious diseases may be the basis for temporarily denying a visa. The adoptive parents must appear at the consulate or embassy for an interview. There is a $260 fee to apply for the visa and a $65 fee for the issuance of the visa.

Citizenship

Part of the adoption process is helping your child become a U.S. citizen. There are several ways this can occur.

Child Citizenship Act

The federal *Child Citizenship Act of 2000* allows an internationally adopted child to automatically become a U.S. citizen. In order for the act to apply, the child must:

- have one U.S. parent (adoptive);
- be legally adopted by this parent;
- be under age 18;
- live with the U.S. parent who has custody of the child; and,
- be admitted to the United States as an immigrant for lawful permanent residence (under an IR-4 Visa).

If these requirements are satisfied, your child will automatically be granted citizenship when the adoption is legal in the United States.

In order for your child to become a citizen, your child's passport (from his or her country of origin) will be stamped with USCIS stamp I-551. You can then apply for a passport for your child (a passport will be your child's proof of citizenship). To apply for a passport, you need the following:

- Form DSP-11, *Application for a Passport*;
- two (2) identical photographs (2 x 2 inches in size);
- the parent's valid identification;
- certified adoption decree (with English translation, if necessary);
- the child's foreign passport with USCIS stamp I-551 or the child's resident alien card; and,
- the fee payment.

Readoption

Because U.S. courts are not required to legally recognize an adoption completed in a foreign country, it is a good idea to adopt your child in your state court, even if you have already completed an adoption process in the child's country of

> **Adoption Answer**
> For more information on the Child Citizenship Act, see:
>
> **http://travel.state.gov/ family/adoption/info/ info_457.html**

origin. At this time, you will obtain a new birth certificate. This will ensure your child has an accurate birth certificate that is acceptable in the United States.

Changes in Adoption Law

The United States may or may not approve changes to international adoption law in the coming years. The *Hague Convention on Intercountry Adoption* is an international document that provides procedures and rules for how international adoptions are handled and processed. If the U.S. does adopt these rules, there will be some changes to the way international adoptions are handled to ensure that the children placed for adoption are truly available. Some experts say the changes will complicate the international adoption process, while others say the changes will provide important protections for all involved in the process.

> **Adoption Answer**
> To read more about proposed changes in how international adoptions are handled and the effects of a change, see:
> **http://www.state.gov/r/ pa/prs/ps/2006/61274.htm**

Dealing with Problems

Most likely your international adoption will go smoothly. Problems can happen, though. If a problem happens while you are in the United States, get in touch with your agency caseworker. If this is unsuccessful, contact your attorney.

Should a problem occur while you are in your child's country of origin, first try to talk with the agency's representative there. They are best able to work out problems since they are familiar with the language and the system in place in that country.

International Adoption Warning Signs

- The agency does not provide references
- The agency will not offer details about its partner agencies in the foreign countries it deals with
- The agency requires a large fee up front, beyond a small application fee
- The agency does not provide escorts, translators, and interpreters when you travel to your child's country of origin
- The agency does not encourage or support you in obtaining a medical evaluation of the child you are assigned before finalizing the adoption

Forms Checklist for International Adoption

- passports (if you will be traveling to meet your child)
- parent's birth certificate — three copies
- marriage certificate — three copies
- divorce decree (if applicable) — three copies

- home study
- fingerprints
- criminal background check
- medical reports — two copies
- reference letters
- Form I-600A and/or I-600, *Petition to Classify Orphan*
- Form I-864, *Affidavit of Support*
- Form IR-3 or IR-4 to apply for a visa

International Agency Questionnaire

Name of Agency _____

Name of Contact Person _____

Date of Interview _____

Questions:

❏ What countries do you have agreements with?

❏ How many children have you placed from each of these countries in the last year?

❏ How long have you worked with each country?

❏ Do the overseas agencies you work with also work with other U.S. agencies?

❏ Who works overseas for your agency?

❏ How do babies come into the programs?

❏ How long will the process take?

❏ If parents must travel to complete the adoption, what arrangements and assistance do you provide for the trip?

❏ Is a travel agency involved?

❏ Is an escort provided?

❑ Is a translator provided?

❑ Can the agency be reached by phone outside of business hours while we are overseas?

❑ What access is provided to the children overseas?

❑ Can the agency provide referrals to Western doctors in the overseas country while we are there, should the need arise?

❑ Are you licensed in this state?

❑ How long have you been doing international adoptions?

❑ If a parent turns down a child, can he or she adopt another child?

❑ What kinds of services do you provide after placement?

Chapter 7

PARENT-INITIATED ADOPTION

A *parent-initiated adoption* is also sometimes called a *private* or *independent adoption*. The adoptive parents locate a birth mother on their own without help from an adoption agency. The reasons for doing this are often because the couple wants to adopt a newborn, the couple does not want to work with an agency, the couple wants more control over the process, the couple already has located a birth mother through their own contacts, or the couple wants more in-depth contact with the birth mother than is often allowed in agency adoptions.

While a parent-initiated adoption can offer a lot of freedom, it has some drawbacks. The main concern is that if you go through the adoption process without an agency involved, you may not be completely aware of all the laws and regulations you need to comply with. Additionally, there is always the chance that the birth mother will change her mind. While this does happen with agency adoptions, the likelihood increases when an agency is not involved to counsel and support the birth mother in making this decision. An agency can often provide an experienced hand that will guide your adoption and help you get over any bumps in the road. On the other hand, a parent-initiated adoption allows you to do things your way, without having to apply to an agency or jump through their hoops. You locate a birth mother with whom you feel a connection and you handle the process yourself (with help from your attorney).

Florida, Kentucky, Massachusetts, Minnesota, New Mexico, and Rhode Island require that you notify the state department of social services when you do a parent-initiated adoption.

Adopting Independently with an Agency

Many parents who choose to locate a birth mother on their own use an agency to handle the actual adoption process itself. To do so, you need to interview agencies in your area and choose one that will handle a parent-initiated adoption. The agency will coordinate the home study, provide counseling, and work with your attorney to complete the adoption process. If you are comfortable working with an agency in this way, it can make the entire process go much more smoothly. There is an intermediary between you and the birth mother and you have someone handling the paperwork on your behalf.

The agency will usually handle payment of the birth mother's expenses, so you need not pay them directly (it will be part of the costs you pay to the agency). However, you will have to pay an agency fee, which you would not pay if you handled the adoption directly with the birth mother.

How to Find a Birth Mother

There are several ways to go about finding a birth mother on your own. First, you may wish to talk to an attorney who is experienced in handling adoptions. Not only will the attorney help you understand the law and how you must go about contacting and reaching an agreement with a birth mother, but many experienced adoption attorneys also have contact with birth mothers seeking adoptive parents for their babies. The attorney may be able to help you find a birth mother. In Florida particularly, adoption attorneys do a lot of facilitation.

Word of mouth is another excellent way to locate a birth mother. Tell your friends and family of your search and ask them to keep their ears open for you. Mention your search to coworkers and acquaintances. Some adoptive parents have business cards made up with their name, number, and a brief description, along with words to the effect of, "We can provide a loving home

> **Adoption Answer**
> For support with and information about private adoption, contact:
>
> **Families for Private Adoption**
> P.O. Box 6375
> Washington, DC 20015
> 202-722-0338
> **www.ffpa.org**

for your baby. Please call us." Hand these out to friends and family and ask them to pass them along to anyone who might be interested. Give some to your gynecologist, family doctor, pastor, rabbi, and so on, if possible. Other couples create a letter to circulate to prospective birth mothers (this is often called a *birth mother letter*) that describes you and your hopes to have a family.

Facilitator

Another option is to use an *adoption facilitator*. This is a professional who works to bring birth mothers and adoptive parents together. Facilitators are not licensed in most states and some states do not allow the use of facilitators. It is a good idea to speak with your attorney before approaching a facilitator. If you do decide to work with one, make sure you check references. Find out how many babies he or she has placed in total as well as in the last year. Make sure that you completely understand any fees involved as well as what the fees would be if a birth mother changes her mind.

The following twelve states have laws specifically regulating payments to a facilitator:

- Alabama
- Colorado
- Louisiana
- Maryland
- Missouri
- South Carolina
- South Dakota
- Tennessee
- Texas
- Utah
- Virginia
- West Virginia

The following states do not permit the use of a facilitator:

- Delaware
- District of Columbia
- Georgia
- Kansas
- Kentucky
- Massachusetts
- Minnesota
- Montana
- Nebraska
- Nevada
- New Mexico
- New York
- Ohio
- Oklahoma
- Oregon

Adoption Answer

Get more information about birth mother letters at:

www.canadaadopts.com/ registry/mistakes.shtml

Costs are usually less than private agency fees because the full range of services is not included in the contract. For example, you would need to pay for the home study, medical exams, counseling, and so on separately.

Advertising

The most popular method employed by adoptive parents to find a birth mother is advertising. You may have seen classified ads in your local paper or in national papers. The following states do not permit advertising by prospective parents:

- Alabama
- California
- Delaware
- Idaho
- Kansas
- Kentucky
- Maine
- Massachusetts
- Montana
- Nevada
- North Dakota
- Ohio
- Texas
- Utah
  (prohibits advertising
  by attorneys or physicians)
- Virginia
  (advertising is very limited)

If your ad starts with the letter "A," it will be near the top of all adoption ads in the paper or on that website. Since most classified ads are short, you will want to spend a lot of time polishing your ad so it contains the most information in the clearest way. Most ads make references to a loving home, financially stable couple, friendly neighborhoods, and other positive factors. Mentioning your professions can help if they are prestigious or sound comforting (such as a doctor, lawyer, nurse, or teacher). The cost of the ad depends on where you place it, but normal classified ad rates usually apply if you are advertising in newspapers. National papers charge higher rates than local papers. Compare the circulation of the papers to determine what prices are best — the

---

Adoption Answer

You can find a list of facilitators online at:

**www.adoption.tk/
professional.htm**

higher the circulation, the more people the ad will reach. Read the classifieds in your local paper to see some ads and get a feel for how you want yours to look.

Ads placed online are another way to locate a birth mother. Before you place an online ad, make sure you find out how many hits the site is receiving each month and ask for references. If you place an ad, you need to make sure your ad complies with all state laws, so be sure to consult with your attorney. You might also want to create a basic Web page about yourselves and your search for a baby, so that birth mothers can see photos and get a lot of information about you up front.

> **Adoption Answer**
> For tips about wording and placing an ad, visit:
>
> **http://adoption.com.ws/ ad.html**

Do not underestimate the power of networking and getting the word out. Tell all your family and friends about your search for a baby and ask them to tell people they know. You might also consider creating a website that showcases your birth mother letter and has photos of you and your home.

Choosing a Birth Mother

Choosing a birth mother is a delicate process. When a birth mother contacts you, your first reaction might be to finalize things before she can change her mind. However, it is important to give yourself time and space to get to know her and to make this important decision. Make up a list of questions you want to ask a potential birth mother. You will not be able to ask her all of these questions the first time you talk, but you will have a written checklist of questions to ask as you have further conversations.

You must decide how comfortable you are with the answers to these questions. For example, if the birth mother smokes, you may wish to find someone else. If the birth mother gives you answers that conflict or that change over time, you may see a red flag. Try to get a sense of what the birth mother is like, what her life is like, and how serious she is about the adoption. You do not want to waste your time with someone who is not at all committed or who might just be trying to get money from you without fulfilling the agreement. You also want to be sure she really is pregnant and really does want to place the baby for adoption. You cannot determine this in one quick conversation. Write down the answers you get and discuss them with your adoption attorney. He or she will be able to guide you as to what kinds of problems to look for. It is easy to get emotionally invested too soon with a birth mother—the thought that this could be your baby can blind you to the warning signs. For this reason, it is important that you work carefully and closely with a professional who can help you see potential problems.

Contact with Birth Mother

Once you are in touch with a possible birth mother, it can be tempting to want to spend a lot of time talking to her and working things out. However, once you have a birth mother who calls you (she should always call you—you should never make the initial call because you do not want to create extra pressure and you must be careful to stay within your state's legal requirements), you need to tell her a little about yourself, find out a little about her (such as when her due date is, how her health is, and if the birth father is in the picture at all), and then have her call your attorney. Your attorney is not able to call her (this creates pressure and she must enter the adoption of her own free will), so you need to stress to her the importance of calling your attorney herself. Your attorney will then proceed from there and make arrangements for medical exams, counseling, and necessary paperwork. You will have many more opportunities to speak with the birth mother before either of you makes a decision about the adoption.

Payments

The average cost of a private adoption is between $10,000 and $15,000. The issue of payments involved in adoptions is a tricky one. It is unrealistic to expect a woman to place her child for adoption without any kind of financial assistance. However, laws about adoption payments were created to make sure that babies are not bought and sold. In most states, adoptive parents are expected to pay for the birth mother's medical expenses (this includes mental health counseling) during the course of her pregnancy. Payments are usually made through third parties — attorneys, facilitators, or agencies that are brought on board after the birth mother has been found.

If the birth mother has health insurance (and many do not), the expenses will be lower. The adoptive parents also handle the baby's expenses from birth. In some states, the law permits the adoptive parents to pay the birth mother's living expenses (basics like rent, utilities, food, and so on) during the last trimester of the pregnancy. Payments are usually permitted if they are *usual and customary* in the state. It is important that you check with your attorney before making any payments to the birth mother so that you are sure you are following your state's law exactly. Adoptive parents can also pay for the birth mother's attorney's fees if she employs an attorney. None of these payments are refundable if the birth mother chooses to keep the baby (except in Idaho, where they are reimbursable).

When you go to court to finalize your adoption, you will have to disclose to the court any payments you have made to the birth mother. For this reason, it is important that you remain within the allowable amounts in your state.

Most states have laws that specify the type of birth parent expenses a prospective adoptive parent is allowed to pay. The actual dollar amount is usually limited to what is reasonable and customary in that state.

The types of expenses most commonly allowed by statute include:

- maternity-related medical and hospital costs;
- temporary living expenses of the mother during pregnancy;
- counseling fees;
- attorney and legal fees;
- guardian ad litem fees;
- travel costs, meals, and lodging when necessary for court appearances or accessing services; and,
- foster care for the child, when necessary.

The following states specify expenses that the adoptive parent is not permitted to pay, such as educational expenses, vehicles, vacations, permanent housing, or any other payment for the monetary gain of the birth parent:

- Illinois
- Kentucky
- Michigan
- Minnesota
- Montana
- New Hampshire
- North Dakota
- Wisconsin

The following states specify that payments for the birth mother's living expenses or counseling costs cannot extend beyond a set time period, from as little as thirty days to as long as six weeks after the child's birth:

- Florida
- Idaho
- Illinois
- Indiana
- Iowa
- Louisiana
- Michigan
- Minnesota
- New Hampshire
- Wisconsin
- New Mexico
- New York
- North Carolina
- North Dakota
- Oklahoma
- Tennessee
- Vermont

Other states set a limit the paid expenses may not exceed:
- Arizona ($1,000)
- Connecticut ($1,500)
- Idaho ($2,000)
- Indiana ($3,000)
- Wisconsin ($1,000)

Iowa allows post placement counseling for sixty days but limits payment of living expenses to thirty days. New York limits payment of living expenses to sixty days prior to the child's birth and thirty days after. Oklahoma allows payments for post placement counseling for up to six months but limits other expenses to two months beyond placement.

Some states do not specify the types of expenses that are not allowed but state that any expense not expressly permitted by law cannot be paid. These states include:

- Delaware
- Iowa
- Louisiana
- Missouri
- New Mexico
- Ohio
- Oregon
- Texas
- Utah
- West Virginia
- Wisconsin

Other states prohibit expenses considered by the court to be unreasonable:

- Arizona
- California
- Florida
- Kansas
- Kentucky
- Missouri

- Ohio
- Oklahoma
- Pennsylvania
- South Carolina
- Virginia

Idaho, in addition to its other restrictions, is the only state that requires reimbursement of expenses to prospective adoptive parents should the birth parent decide not to place the child for adoption.

Counseling

Before you agree to anything, it is essential that the birth mother attend counseling. An initial evaluation will help reveal any negative feelings she has about the placement. Ongoing counseling will help her deal with the inevitable emotions she will face as she goes through the pregnancy and delivery and the adjustment period afterwards. Your attorney can assist the birth mother in locating a counselor experienced in adoption. You will pay for the cost of this counseling.

Counseling can also be helpful for the adoptive parents. As you wait for your baby to be born, you will also face anxiety, doubt, and fear. A counselor can help you work through the process and stay focused on the goal of adding a child to your family.

Counseling should be part of your agreement with the birth mother. It is a warning sign if a birth mother is resistant to counseling. At the very least, you must have a psychological evaluation done so that you know what you are dealing with. There are some instances in which counseling might not be necessary, but in general, it is considered necessary for all adoptions. Counseling is usually done separately for

> **Adoption Answer**
>
> For referrals to counselors, visit the American Psychological Association at:
>
> **www.apa.org**

the adoptive parents and birth mother, but there are some instances in which going together can be helpful, particularly if there are issues you need to work out or if you are trying to create a plan for how you will have contact after the birth.

If your birth mother lives in your area, you can provide her with a list of counselors and even offer to drive her there. If she lives far away from you, you can still put together a list of counselors in her area.

Waiting for Your Child to Be Born

When you use parent-initiated adoption, you are more closely in tune with what is happening with the birth mother as the pregnancy develops and you may have the opportunity to see or speak to her throughout the pregnancy. This relationship may be very close or not close at all. Each adoption is different and you will have to work within your comfort zone as well as that of the birth mother. Your attorney or adoption agency can be helpful intermediaries in this situation and can help communicate some basic rules for contact.

Some birth mothers and adoptive parents make arrangements for the adoptive parents to be present at the birth. You will need to work this out with your birth mother in advance. If you are present at the hospital, you will want to make sure the staff is aware you are the adoptive parents so that you can have access to the birth mother and baby. The birth mother will need to give her specific consent to this since the baby belongs to her until the placement occurs. If she does not consent, you have no right to see her or the baby.

Paperwork

As with any other adoption, the adoption is not finalized and complete until the waiting period is up, which varies depending on the state the child is born in. (See Chapter 5 for more information.) Any agreements you make with the birth mother before this are all subject to revocation of her consent to the adoption. While you and the birth mother will sign documents (which will vary by state) indicating that you consent to the adoption, this can all change if the birth mother changes her mind within the revocation period. If the birth mother lives in a different state, you will need an attorney in her state and one in your own. Select an attorney in your home state first and he or she can then locate an attorney in the birth mother's state.

It is essential that you use an attorney to draft all the adoption documents. You will want to be sure that the papers you and the birth mother sign and present to the court are correct for your state and legally acceptable to the court. The birth mother must have her own attorney and cannot use yours. The court may scrutinize a parent-initiated adoption more closely than an agency adoption to be sure that state laws about payment and consent have been carefully followed.

Once the waiting period concludes, the adoption is legalized and you become parents. (See Chapter 3 for more information about adoption paperwork and about birth certificates.)

Adjustment Period

After the adoption has been finalized in your state, the legal process is over for you, but the adjustment process will probably still continue. You will need to find a way to manage contact with the birth mother. Hopefully this was something you discussed and worked out with her while you were waiting for the birth, but do not be surprised if things do not go as planned. Some birth mothers who wanted regular contact may find it is less painful to get some distance and move on with their lives. Other birth mothers who thought they would want little contact may find they want more than originally thought.

Keep in mind that you are now the legal parent of this child and you are the one making the decisions. It is a good idea to try to be fair to the birth mother simply because this is what is right to do for your child, but you must make the ultimate decision about what is best for your child and what works for your family.

Dealing with Problems

If you experience problems in your parent-initiated adoption, it is important that you work closely with your attorney to resolve them. One of the biggest problems is the adoption falling through. Should the birth mother change her mind, you have no recourse, so you must always approach the situation with a careful eye and make sure everything is completely in line before you commit both financially and emotionally to the adoption. Counseling is a very important way to make sure the adoption is the right one. A good counselor can help the birth mother through the difficult process she is facing and can also help you deal with the ups and downs of the process.

Birth Mother Warning Signs

- She won't give you an address or phone number.
- She wants money up front for rent or expenses.
- You have no documentation that she is actually pregnant.
- The birth mother wants to bring the baby to you, instead of you coming to the hospital.

- The birth mother misses meetings with you, or you have never seen her in person.
- The birth mother does not want to talk to your attorney or any other adoption professional.
- Her story seems to change about the pregnancy, her situation, or her needs.
- She says she is expecting twins. Always get proof of this.
- She agrees to the adoption too quickly without really getting to know you, and seems extremely enthusiastic.
- She refuses to see a counselor.
- The dates she gives don't add up.

Facilitator Warning Signs

- The facilitator will not give you an address or phone number for the business.
- He or she becomes offended or insulted when you ask pertinent questions meant to protect yourself.
- What you have been told does not match what is in the contract you are given.
- The facilitator requires large amounts of money up front (beyond a small application fee).
- The facilitator is difficult to reach and does not respond quickly to your calls or emails.
- He or she will not provide references.

Facilitator Questionnaire

Name of Facilitator _____

Date of Interview _____

Questions:

❑ How many adoptions have you placed in the last year?

❑ Can you provide references?

❑ How long have you been doing this?

❑ How many clients do you work with each year?

❑ How do you find birth mothers?

❑ How do you evaluate birth mothers?

❑ What is your success rate?

❑ How many of your birth mothers change their minds?

❑ What are your fees?

❑ What does your contract look like?

❑ What portion of fees are refundable if the birth mother changes her mind?

Potential Birth Mother Questionnaire

Name of Birth Mother _____

Date of Interview _____

Questions:

❑ Why are you placing this child for adoption?

❑ How far along are you?

❑ What is your due date?

❑ Who knows about your pregnancy?

- ❏ Who is the birth father?
- ❏ Is he aware of the pregnancy?
- ❏ Have you seen a doctor?
- ❏ Who is your doctor?
- ❏ Do you have any medical conditions?
- ❏ Do you want an open adoption, and if so, what do you mean by that term?
- ❏ What are you looking for in the adoptive parents?
- ❏ Do you have a job?
- ❏ What do you do?
- ❏ Do you smoke, drink, or take any medication?
- ❏ Are you taking prenatal vitamins?
- ❏ What is your family medical history?
- ❏ What is your ethnic heritage?
- ❏ How old are you?
- ❏ What education do you have?
- ❏ Where do you live?
- ❏ Who do you live with?
- ❏ Are you in a relationship? Does your partner know about the pregnancy?
- ❏ How do you support yourself?
- ❏ Do you have other children?
- ❏ Have you placed any other children for adoption?
- ❏ Have you talked with a counselor or adoption agency about placement?
- ❏ What kind of support system do you have in place?
- ❏ Can you provide photos of yourself and other family members?
- ❏ How long have you known about the pregnancy?

Chapter 8

SINGLE-PARENT ADOPTION

Single-parent adoption is more commonplace than it ever used to be. Every state now recognizes that a good home does not depend on having two parents present and allows adoption by singles. You do not need to be married to be a parent, and many, many people are not.

Considerations for Single-Parent Adoption

When you seek to adopt as a single, the primary concern that agencies and social workers will have is that you have a support system in place. Before seeking to adopt, give some thought to who will help you; who can provide child care; and, how you will provide role models of both sexes for your child. Family and friends provide excellent backup as well as opposite-sex role models.

When making the decision to adopt as a single person, it is important to realize the weight of the decision. A child will be completely dependent on you. You also will carry the financial and emotional burden alone—as well as the logistics of raising the child. Before you adopt, it is important to carefully think through all the possible scenarios—how your child will be cared for while you work; how you will afford the additional expenses; who you will turn to for help; how you will continue to have a social life; who will care for your child should you die; and so on. Remember, there are many single parents who raise biological or adoptive children alone, so while it presents some challenges, it is most definitely something you can do.

Bias Against Single Parents

While single-parent adoption is permitted in all states, some agencies and social workers continue to hold a bias against prospective single adoptive parents. If you encounter this kind of bias, it is best to confront it head-on and provide a lot of information for the agency or worker about your support system and deal with their concerns up front. There is often particular bias against single men seeking to adopt, based on misguided suspicions about pedophilia. Single men may have to work harder to convince agencies and social workers about their reasons for wanting to adopt, but they have the same rights to adopt as anyone else. No one can turn you down for adoption simply because you are not married; however, other excuses may be used to discourage you. If you are confronting bias, it is a signal that you need to seek out another, less judgmental agency.

> **Adoption Answer**
>
> For information and support, contact:
>
> **National Council for Single Adoptive Parents**
> P.O. Box 55
> Wharton, NJ 07885
> http://encyclopedia.
> adoption.com/entry/
> National-Council-for-
> Single-Adoptive-
> Parents/244/1.html

There is also often an assumption that a single seeking to adopt must be gay. (See Chapter 9 for information about gay and lesbian adoption.) While you may be asked about your sexual orientation as part of the home study process, it should not matter what your orientation is as long as you have a lifestyle that is conducive to parenting.

Home Studies

You may need to work a little harder than married couples to get through the home study. You will need to show the social worker that you have thought through all the possibilities and have come up with a plan or with solutions to deal with them. Generally, it will be important to demonstrate a support network of family and friends who can step in to help. You should show that you have given thought to child care and that you know how to arrange your finances so that you can handle the extra expenses. You should also create a plan to take some time off when the adoption happens so you can bond with your child and ease the adjustment. Make it clear that you have planned this very well and that you feel secure in your ability to handle it. You will also need to show that you have a plan in place so that others are available to care for your child should you become ill, tied up at work, or have to go out of town. You should also mention that you plan to have a will drawn up that will name a guardian for your child. It is perfectly okay to say you will be dating while you raise your child and it is also perfectly okay to have a boyfriend or girlfriend.

Laws Governing Single-Parent Adoption

All states permit singles to adopt. However, there are a few catches. In Utah, where adoption by singles is permitted, anyone who is unmarried and cohabiting is not permitted to adopt. Florida and Mississippi do not permit adoption by anyone who is homosexual. (See Chapter 9 for more information.) Korea is currently the one foreign country that does not permit adoption of its children by singles.

Protecting Your Family

Single parents who adopt should consider purchasing disability insurance and life insurance to provide for their family's financial security. Disability insurance will guarantee you an income should you become unable to work, and life insurance provides for your child should something happen to you. It is also a good idea to have a well-thought-out investment plan, so that you can create some financial security. Raising a child is an expensive proposition and some single parents find that it is difficult to continue to work full time or afford day care costs. It most definitely can be done though, so it is a good idea to create a financial plan for your new family. It will also be essential to execute a will naming a guardian for your child. You may wish to execute this will before your adoption is finalized. (There was a case in which a woman had a fatal accident as she was returning home with her newly adopted child and since she had no will, the court had to decide on a guardian.)

Raising Your Child

With more and more people divorcing and singles adopting or having children without a partner, the single-parent family is no longer an oddity. Few people will give your adoption a second thought. However, there are some people who will simply not understand that your child does not have another parent. They will assume you must be divorced or not living with your child's other parent. "Where's his father?" and "What do you mean she only has one parent?" are examples of the types of questions you may encounter.

As you raise your child, you will encounter some bumps in the road. There is just one of you and you cannot be in all places at all times. Conflicts will come up, but if you have a support network in place, your child will be well cared for. You want family and friends you can rely on in emergencies, as well as in the day-to-day logistics of parenting.

Make sure that you leave room in your life for friends and for dating, if that is what you are interested in. You may be a parent, but you are still a person. You should be able to continue to work hard at your career, have fun, and spend some money on yourself. Parenting is not all about sacrifice.

Realize that although single parenting is easy for you to accept, it may not be easy for other people to accept. You may find yourself explaining more times than you wish that no, your child does not have another parent and no, you are not widowed or divorced. As your child grows, spend some time explaining to him or her the different kinds of families and how you came to be a single parent. The story of how you and your child became a family is an important one and has just as much value as the story in any two-parent family.

Children of single-parent families thrive and do just as well as children from families with two parents. In short, adopting a child on your own does not provide any particular roadblocks or problems for your child, unless you create them.

Chapter 9

GAY AND LESBIAN ADOPTION

In recent years, the laws about same-sex couple adoptions have become more encompassing, as more and more states have accepted gay couples as adoptive parents. There are several paths to consider when you and your partner want to become parents.

Single-Parent Adoption

If you are gay and single, your sexual orientation should not come into play with adoption. The information contained in Chapter 8 details the process and procedures you should follow as a single person seeking to adopt. It is only when you are seeking to adopt as a couple that the situation is handled differently.

Second-Parent Adoption

If one partner has a child (that is his or her natural child or is a child he or she adopted) and the other partner would like to adopt the child, a second-parent adoption procedure can be used. (See Chapter 4 for more information about second-parent adoptions.) Second-parent adoptions are also the process you need to use in many states if you and your partner want to adopt a child together. Because in most states, gay couples cannot adopt together, one parent must adopt the child first and then the partner must do a second-parent adoption. There are some restrictions on same-sex, second-parent adoption, since it is not permitted in all states. The areas that permit same-sex, second-parent adoption include:

- California
- Connecticut
- District of Columbia
- Illinois
- Massachusetts

- New Jersey
- New York
- Pennsylvania
- Vermont

Other states have permitted some same-sex, second-parent adoptions, but do not have a clear-cut policy. These states include:

- Alabama
- Alaska
- Delaware
- Georgia
- Hawaii
- Indiana
- Iowa
- Louisiana
- Maryland
- Michigan

- Minnesota
- Nevada
- New Hampshire
- New Mexico
- Ohio
- Oregon
- Rhode Island
- Texas
- Washington

Florida completely disallows adoption by gays.

Utah law does not allow unmarried people who are cohabiting to adopt. Although the laws that permit second-parent adoption treat it as a separate process, in reality, gay couples are really adopting together. Yes, one partner must be the one to initially adopt the child and then the other partner can do a second-parent adoption, but these are just legal terms and processes and you should not get too bogged down with them. You are adopting together and you will parent together. There is no reason to think of it in any other way. The American Academy of Pediatrics formally supports second-parent adoption by gay partners. Hopefully the tide is turning, and soon more states will have clear-cut second-parent adoptions for gay couples.

Couple Adoption

Gay couples can adopt a child together, simultaneously, in the District of Columbia, Massachusetts, New York, New Jersey, Vermont, and California. Most other states have laws that are not clear on this issue.

However, this does not mean gay couples cannot adopt in most states. The best procedure to use in other states is a two-step adoption. In the first step, one partner adopts the child alone. He or she can use an agency or independent adoption—whatever method works best for him or her. Once that adoption is complete, then the other partner can seek a second-parent adoption of the child in those states that permit second-parent adoptions by gay partners.

Adoption Answer

Read your state adoption laws at:

www.lambdalegal.org

International Adoption

Gay adoption is not permitted by any international country. However, this does not mean a gay single or couple cannot adopt. Single-parent international adoption is possible if you are not open about your sexuality. You simply do not mention you are gay and your adoption proceeds as it would for any single person. If you are a couple, the child can then be adopted by the other parent via a second-parent adoption procedure.

Finding Gay-Friendly Adoption Agencies

To find a gay-friendly agency, talk to other same-sex couples who have adopted. Contact your local gay pride organization and ask for information about agencies they are aware of.

If you and/or your partner are seeking an agency adoption, it will be important to carefully question the agency about their policies regarding same-sex adoption. Listen not only to the official, written

Adoption Answer

For a list of countries with policies against gay adoption, visit:

http://adoption.about. com/od/gaylesbian/ a/gayadopt.htm

policy, but also to the nuances you pick up when talking to agency employees, in the literature you receive, and in all of your contacts with the agency. You want an agency that is comfortable with you and that will work to the best of its ability to place a child with you. If the birth mothers play a role in selecting adoptive parents, you will have a second barrier to deal with. Each birth mother will have her own preferences and opinions. If the agency policy is accepting and welcoming, make sure you use one of the social workers employed by or recommended by the

Adoption Answer

The Human Rights Campaign offers a database of gay-friendly adoption agencies at:

www.hrc.org

Click on "Adopting through an Agency."

agency to avoid any potential bias when you go through the home study process. During the home study process, it will be important to demonstrate that your relationship is solid and committed. If you have registered with any domestic partner registries, obtained a civil union or gay marriage license, or completed any affidavits for employers about your relationship (often required in order to access health benefits for a partner), it is important to share this information with your social worker. You should also mention a commitment ceremony or wedding, if you had one.

It is up to you if you choose to share the fact that you are gay. If you and a partner live together as spouses, it will be very difficult to cover that fact up during your home study. Anyone who lives in your home with you must be part of your home study and it is likely it will be obvious to the social worker that you truly are spouses, not roommates.

Public agencies are always a safe bet if your state has laws specifically permitting adoption by gays. There are always children available for adoption through public agencies, although they are usually not infants and may have special needs. (See Chapter 2 for more information about public agencies.)

Raising an Adoptive Child in a Gay Family

Unfortunately, there is still discrimination against gay families, no matter how they are formed. As you raise your child, you will need to be on the lookout for schools, child care facilities, camps, and organizations that will accept and welcome your child and your family. Keep an eye out for literature that refers to *parents* instead of *mothers and fathers*. Ask about *gay-straight alliances* (GSAs), school organizations that strive to support and include all students from all families. (The 1984 *Equal Access Law* held that if a school receives federal funds and has a limited open forum, meaning they allow other non-curriculum-based groups to meet and use school resources, then the school cannot discriminate about which types of groups the school allows or supports.)

As you raise your child, you will find ways to talk to your child about being gay. Your child will have questions about your life, but for the most part it will feel completely natural to

> **Adoption Answer**
>
> The Gay, Lesbian, and Straight Educational Network can provide more information about school inclusiveness. Contact them at:
>
> **212-727-0135**
>
> or
>
> **www.glsen.org**

Adoption Answer

For information and support about gay parenting, contact:

Family Pride Coalition
P.O. Box 65327
Washington, DC 20035
202-331-5015
www.familypride.org

Adoption Answer

Help your child understand and deal with social reactions and help him or her understand the issues and your point of view by sharing books, such as those on the list created by Children of Lesbians and Gays Everywhere at:

www.colage.org/pubs/ books_for_kids.pdf

him or her, and your child will grow up knowing that families come in all different sizes, shapes, and configurations. You and your child will probably encounter discrimination and ignorance, so it is important that you find ways to talk about this and cope with it together.

Spending time with other gay families or helping your child find support is important. Your child will need role models from the opposite sex. Work with other gay or lesbian families to provide this kind of support. You can also make sure your child spends time with straight family and friends so that he or she comes to know and love people of all types.

If you and your partner adopt your child together, you may encounter ignorance and unpleasantness at times. Many people are still unaware of the fact that gay couples can adopt children together and be legal parents together—some people do not even know that gay marriages are legal in some places. You may have to offer proof to get someone to believe you—such as showing a birth certificate to a school or day care center. Try to keep in mind that everything you do makes it easier for those gay couples or singles who come after you, so every bit of education or eye-opening you do has meaning and purpose. Your main goal is to raise a happy and healthy child and if education is a side effect of that, it's an added benefit.

Chapter 10

KINSHIP ADOPTION

Kinship adoption occurs when the birth parents are unable to care for a child (or are no longer in the child's life) and some member of the child's family seeks to adopt him or her. Kinship adoptions are an important way to provide children with continuity of family and culture. They are also less stressful for the child and birth parents because family ties are not completely severed, just rearranged. Many times when a parent becomes unable to care for a child, the grandparents or other relatives step in and become caregivers for the child. However, these family caregivers need to have legal authority to make decisions for the child in order to be effective caregivers. Kinship adoptions also allow children to have continuing contact with their birth parent(s) or to at least have access to information about them, while giving them the security of a legal parent who is in a position to provide proper care.

Types of Kinship Adoptions

The most common kinship adoption is adoption by the child's grandparents. This often happens when the birth parents are young or unable to care for the child. This often starts as an informal arrangement and becomes legal only by necessity, when schools require proof of guardianship or parenthood. Kinship adoption also commonly includes adoption by aunts or uncles.

When talking about kinship adoption, it is important to understand that there are two kinds. There are kinship adoptions that are given special treatment by states, which simplifies the process. Then there are kinship adoptions that are treated as regular adoptions, but in which the child happens to be related to the adoptive parents in some way. While this second kind of adoption can be wonderful for helping a child maintain ties and identity, it has no special legal status. (This chapter discusses kinship adoptions that are given special recognition by the states.)

Adoption vs. Guardianship

When a grandparent or other relative assumes the care for a child, a fast way to obtain authority and legality is through a *guardianship* process. Guardianship is a legal decision by a court that one person should have legal and financial decision-making power over another person, such as a child or person who is mentally incompetent.

Guardianship is not the same as custody or legal parentage because the court maintains the final legal authority over the child. The guardian remains in charge of the child only as long as the court approves. Children cared for by a guardian do not usually qualify for the guardian's health care plan and cannot inherit from their guardians (unless specified in a will), but adoptive children can. Guardianship usually only happens with the consent of the parent or if the child has been placed into foster care and the state social services department consents to the guardianship. Because guardianship is not permanent, many relatives prefer to seek an adoption as a final resolution for the child and themselves. Guardianship stays in place only as long as the court decrees and can be easily undone. Adoption offers the child permanency and creates a parent-child bond in a way that guardianship cannot, and it cannot be reversed by a court. However, adoption legally changes who is the child's parent, whereas with guardianship, the child's relationship to his or her biological parents remains intact and unchanged.

Standby Guardianship

A variation on guardianship, *standby guardianship* is a fairly recent development. This type of guardianship was developed so that parents with a terminal illness could establish a guardian who could immediately step in with legal authority once they pass away. A parent can name a guardian for their child in a will, but this will not take effect until the will is approved by the court, which can take some time. A standby guardianship puts a guardian in place immediately upon the parent's death. This type of guardianship provides much needed stability for the child at this difficult time.

> ### Adoption Answer
>
> The AARP Grandparent Information Center is an excellent resource for grandparents who are raising or planning on adopting their grandchildren. Find information on it at:
>
> **www.aarp.org/families/grandparents/raising_grandchild**

Custody vs. Adoption

It is difficult for a relative, even a grandparent, to take a parent to court and seek custody or the right to adopt the child. Grandparents' rights are considered secondary to parental rights and only in the most extreme cases will a grandparent be given custody of a child against a parent's wishes. However, this does happen, particularly in cases where a grandparent is already providing care for the child. Getting custody of your grandchild through your local family court is not the same as adoption. In a custody case, you are given legal authority to act as that child's parent—to have him or her live with you and to make decisions about the child's life. However, this is not the same as adoption, in which you actually become the child's parent. It is also important to note that custody can be changed at a later date if the court decides it is warranted, but an adoption cannot be undone.

Custody is a less permanent solution, but may be preferable if you are waiting for a biological parent to kick an addiction, clean up his or her life, or overcome some other obstacles. If the parent consents to your taking the child, guardianship is the process you should follow.

Adoption vs. Foster Care

Some kinship adoptions are done from kinship foster care arrangements. Kinship foster care is a wonderful alternative to traditional foster care, but again it fails to offer permanency to the child. While foster care children receive state subsidies, adoptive children do not receive subsidies or do not receive the same amount of subsidy, making this a disadvantage to adopting your kinship foster care child. Foster care also involves supervision by the state, whereas adoption is not supervised once it is finalized. You need to meet your state's qualifications to become a foster parent.

Notice and Consent

Notice and consent laws apply to kinship adoptions, just as they do to stepparent adoptions. (See Chapter 4 for more information.) However, in most instances, the birth parents provide consent and often suggest the adoption. The same revocation rules apply as for all adoptions. If the child is of the age specified by the state, he or she must provide consent as well.

Kinship Agreements

Some birth parents create *kinship agreements* with the adoptive parents to continue a child's bonds with family members and to reinforce cultural identity. Also known as *post-adoption contracts* or *cooperative adoption agreements,* these agreements continue the child's relationship with the birth parents. Sometimes these agreements are informal understandings within the family. While the legal relationship between the child and birth parents has ended and the adoptive parents become the legal parents, the family has an understanding that the child will know who his or her mother or father is and may even continue to refer to him or her that way.

Some states formally recognize kinship agreements and make them part of the adoption decree. The court can enforce the agreements and makes sure the parties comply with them. However, failure to comply with the agreement usually cannot provide the basis for revoking or invalidating the adoption. The agreements are important because they provide a lasting link to the biological family. There is usually no simple compliance mechanism because the only solution would be to undo the adoption. That is not a solution that will help the children in the long run.

Kinship agreements are forward-thinking arrangements meant to better a child's life. Sometimes they do not work out, but it is usually in the child's best interest to try to follow them if one might work in your situation.

Often, if a child is over the age of twelve, he or she must consent to the kinship agreement. States that enforce kinship agreements include:

- Arizona
- California
- Connecticut (only when the child was adopted from foster care)
- Florida
- Indiana (only when the child is age 2 or older)
- Louisiana
- Maryland
- Massachusetts
- Minnesota
- Montana
- Nebraska (only when the child is adopted from foster care)
- Nevada

- New Hampshire
- New Mexico
- New York
- Oklahoma
- Oregon
- Rhode Island
- Texas
- Vermont (only in stepparent adoptions)
- Washington
- West Virginia

Some birth parents fail to understand the level of access granted to them by kinship agreements. These agreements never give a birth parent the right to change his or her mind about the adoption, permanently take the child, or make decisions for the child. The adoption is first and foremost always in place. Kinship agreements simply provide a framework for giving the child a lasting connection with the birth parents or other relatives. Kinship agreements can also be important if siblings are adopted into different homes or families. It is often difficult to find adoptive parents that can accept sibling groups, particularly if there are more than two siblings. If siblings are to be adopted, it is often done separately. The court can issue a kinship order, requiring that the siblings continue to see each other and be part of each other's lives. These types of orders are very important, because otherwise, the siblings could completely lose touch with each other.

Agency Involvement

Kinship adoptions can be done privately (without an agency) or with an agency. Often the agency involved is the local public agency. If the agency places a foster child with a relative, the agency will continue to be involved throughout the process of freeing the child for adoption or obtaining consent from the birth parents. (See Chapter 2 for more information about agency adoptions.)

Court Proceedings

The court process for kinship adoptions is no different from those for other adoptions, except that there may not be an agency involved. (See Chapter 3 for more information about court proceedings.) Some states require home studies, while others do not. Additionally, judges are sometimes permitted to waive the requirement. If a home study is required, it is done by the state department of social services and is normally brief. Home studies are often not required for kinship adoptions, or they can usually be waived by the judge.

Finalization

Once a kinship adoption is complete, the new birth certificate will be issued listing the adoptive parents, even if there is a kinship agreement in place allowing the child contact with the birth parents. (See Chapter 3 for information about birth certificates.) Kinship adoptions provide children with stability and security while maintaining a full sense of family history and connections.

Coping with Kinship Adoption

Raising a child you have adopted through a kinship adoption has benefits and drawbacks. A huge benefit is that the child was already part of your family and was probably familiar to you before you adopted. This makes the adjustment process simpler for everyone. However, often children adopted through kinship adoptions can be confused about the change in their family—it is still familiar but not the same.

It is best if you talk with your child about what the adoption means. It may also be a good idea to draw some clear lines about what to call

Adoption Answer

Generations United is an organization that provides information and support to kinship caregivers. Their website contains information about financial assistance, respite care, support, and housing. It also has detailed information on specific state laws about kinship care and adoption. Contact them at:

Generations United
1333 H Street, NW
Suite 500 W
Washington, DC 20005
202-289-3979
www.gu.org

Adoption Answer

If you are a grandparent who has adopted your grandchild, you can find help and support through websites such as:

www.grandsplace.com

and

**www.grandparent
again.com**

you. Do you want to be Mom or Dad or will you ask your child to continue calling you whatever he or she did before the adoption? You have to reach a decision that is right for your own family.

Additionally, while it is wonderful that your child may continue to know and have contact with his or her birth parents, as well as the rest of the birth family, there is potential for conflict with birth parents who think they should still have a say in the child's life or birth relatives who do not understand their new roles. It is important to be clear with the entire family about how this adoption is going to work and what the rules are going to be. It takes time to allow the entire family to adjust to a kinship adoption and for everyone to accept their new roles. Kinship agreements can be helpful for laying out roles and boundaries, but as an adoptive parent, you must make certain everyone understands that you are your child's parent, and as such you will be making all decisions for him or her from now on.

Chapter 11

ADULT ADOPTION

When most people think about adoption, they think about adoption of a child. In fact, it is possible to adopt another adult. There are various reasons why an *adult adoption* might occur. Some people develop very strong parent-child type bonds with people they are not related to. If their legal parents are deceased or they have broken ties with them, an adoption is a way to formalize the bond they feel with each other and also to provide inheritance rights. Another common instance of adult adoption is when a man believes himself to be another person's biological parent, but it has never been proven (or cannot be proven) and there is no other legal father. In these instances, it can provide closure for both parties and legalize a relationship they believe already exists.

Adult adoption is also common in a stepparent situation. The stepparent may have wished to adopt the stepchild but the other legal parent would not consent. Once the child becomes an adult, the adoption can occur without the consent of the biological father, and is a way to legalize the parent-child relationship that developed with the stepparent. Adult adoption has also occasionally been used by gay and lesbian couples as a way to legalize a relationship where marriage is not permitted. The adoption gives the couple legal ties, including inheritance rights and the ability to make medical decisions for each other. However, most gay couples find that this does not provide them with the type of legal bond they are seeking. There are other alternatives that work better, such as Vermont civil unions, domestic partnerships, and ongoing growth in gay marriage rights.

Evaluating the Need for Adult Adoption

If you are considering adult adoption, you need to first think about what your reasons are for the adoption. The emotional and psychological benefits can be worthwhile. Some people choose an adult adoption to provide a legal link so that they need not worry about *inheritance.* Inheritance issues can easily be dealt with by having a simple will drawn up, so this should not be used as the main reason for this type of adoption. Although you can use a will to direct your inheritance, dealing with survivor benefits is another matter. Only a legal child can receive survivor benefits or sue on behalf of a deceased parent.

Another reason for adult adoption is if a person has special needs. If a person who has special needs loses his or her parents, he or she may need someone else who can step in and fill that role for them. This would include being able to make medical and financial decisions for the person. In this situation, the adoption can also provide some much-needed emotional security as well for the adoptee.

> **Adoption Answer**
>
> For support and information on readoption in situations where the child was placed for adoption in a coercive situation, see **www.adoptingback.com.**

There are also situations in which a biological parent had no choice but to place a child for adoption, or in which parental rights were terminated against the parent's wishes. In these cases, readoption by the biological parent can be an important way to correct what both parties might see as a big mistake.

Restrictions

Not all states permit the adoption of adults. Alabama and Ohio allow this type of adoption only if the adoptee is permanently physically or mentally disabled. Ohio also permits adult adoption if the adoptee is a foster child or stepchild. Arizona, Idaho, and Illinois permit adult adoption only if there has been an ongoing parent-child relationship for a period of time.

New Jersey does not specifically permit adult adoption, but does not ban it either. Colorado permits adult adoption only for adoptees between the ages of 18 and 21.

Massachusetts permits adult adoption, but requires that the adoptee be younger than the adoptive parent, unless an aunt, uncle, spouse, or sibling is doing the adopting. Virginia has a similar law, but allows adoption by aunt, uncle, or stepparent, or by anyone else for a good reason if the adoptive parent is fifteen years older than the person being adopted. Nevada also requires that the adoptee be younger than the adoptive parent.

Consent

Both the adoptee and the adoptive parent must consent to the adoption. There is no consent required by the adoptee's legal or biological parents, or this requirement can be waived by the court.

Legal Procedure

If your state permits adoption of adults, a different set of forms is most likely used. Home studies and background checks are not required in most states, since the adult being adopted is presumed to be able to evaluate the situation on his or her own—although this may differ if the adoptee has mental disabilities. The legal process is relatively fast for normal adults since there is no need to wait for the intensive checking to be completed. A court date will be held and both the adoptive parent and adoptee will be present and provide consent to the adoption. If the adoptee has special needs, the court will appoint a *guardian ad litem* who will evaluate the situation and make recommendations to the court. The process will take longer when dealing with a person with special needs.

Effect of Adult Adoption

When an adult adoption is finalized, the adoptive parent becomes the adoptee's legal parent. The adoptee may no longer inherit from his or her biological parents (unless one of them is listed on the birth certificate as a second parent or unless a bequest is specifically made in a will). The adoptee also can no longer inherit from other biological relatives unless a will specifically provides for this. The new legal parents take the role of a parent in every way, which can mean making medical and financial decisions for a special needs adult.

Chapter 12

EMBRYO DONATION/ ADOPTION

Embryo adoption or donation is a new alternative to traditional adoption. This type of adoption is the donation of a fertilized embryo by a couple to another couple, who use the embryos in fertility treatments. These embryos or zygotes are usually extras that have resulted when other couples have undergone fertility procedures, such as IVF. The egg has been fertilized and has begun to develop into a baby (sometimes also called a *zygote*—but technically an embryo is a few days older than a zygote). These embryos are frozen by the couple for use in later fertility cycles. When this couple determines they no longer need these embryos, because they have gotten pregnant, stopped trying, or decided they no longer need these embryos, the embryos can be donated to a mother or couple who would like to have a child, but are unable to do so on their own.

Because fertility procedures usually produce more zygotes than are safe to implant at once, couples undergoing these procedures often freeze the extras. The original intent may be to save them for later cycles if the current one is unsuccessful. The couple may also intend to save them in order to have biological siblings for their child later.

Although there are many couples undergoing fertility treatment and producing many extra zygotes, few actually donate them to other couples. There are over 400,000 embryos being kept frozen in the United States. Many couples eventually dispose of their excess embryos. Many others donate them for research. Once they have gone through the very long and difficult process of harvesting the eggs and having them fertilized and frozen, these frozen embryos are very valuable to them and it is difficult to give them away after they worked so hard to create them.

> **Adoption Answer**
>
> For more information on embryo adoption, see the National Embryo Donation Center's website at **www.embryodonation.org**.

Embryo donation is an alternative to disposal or research use. There have been at least fifty-three children born using embryo donation, according to a recent survey by the Embryo Donation Task Force. Compared to the number of children adopted each year or conceived using other artificial reproductive technology (ART), this is very small. However, it is an option to consider and one that may best fit the needs of some couples.

There are two types of embryo donation. The terminology used is important because it has implications for the pro-life and pro-choice movements. If it is known as embryo adoption, it gives more weight to the argument that embryos are humans. *Embryo donation* is the term used more often since it is a more neutral term.

When you accept an embryo donation, it is like adopting a child from birth, the only difference being that you or your partner actually carries the pregnancy. You have no idea what your child will be like — and you also do not know if the embryo will actually implant. It is likely that your child will have siblings in the world that you will never know about, since most embryo donations come from other couples undergoing fertility treatments with the purpose of having a child.

However, unlike with traditional adoption, neither you nor the birth parents know anything about each other and you in no way choose each other. You are instead matched by a fertility clinic, and because there are so few embryos donated to other couples, there is rarely any kind of choice in the matter. Unlike traditional adoption, your child is legally yours from the moment of birth, and there are no home studies, paperwork, court appearances, or involvement by anyone other than your physician in the process. No one even needs to know you have accepted a donated embryo if you do not wish to tell them. Embryo donation has been in the news recently. The federal government invested $1 million in a public awareness campaign to improve awareness about it as an option, while at the same time opposing the use of embryos for research. While this is a political power play, it has helped to bring the issue of embryo donation to the forefront. Embryo donation has benefits and detriments. The following list looks at its pros and cons.

Embryo Donation

Pros:
- It is much faster than adoption.
- The intended parents completely control the pregnancy.
- The intended mother gives birth to the baby and can nurse.
- Genetic siblings are possible if there are enough embryos from the donor couple.
- The process offers greater privacy than adoption.
- Complete genetic screening is done on the embryos.
- Complete medical information about biological parents is provided.
- You do not have the costs involved in an adoption.
- There is no paperwork involved.
- You are guaranteed an infant.
- There is no qualification process.

• The legal risk is low since the donor couple never knows about the pregnancy and cannot attempt to get custody of the child or otherwise interfere.

Cons:
• Donors tend to be people who have fertility problems themselves, so the embryos may have some problems.
• There is very little selection or choice since there are few embryos available.
• You cannot meet the biological parents and may not even see a photo of them.
• Donors tend to be older, which may cause problems with the embryos.
• Your child may have full genetic siblings in the world without your knowledge.
• It will be very difficult for your child to locate his or her genetic parents in the future.
• You have the expenses involved with IVF treatments, as well the necessary hormone injections.
• You pay the full expenses even if the IVF is not successful.
• There is a high rate of failure to implant (only about 24% successfully do so).

Finding a Donor

Some clinics arrange embryo donation and match donors and recipients themselves—with attention paid to ethnicity and physical characteristics. Recipients usually do not have the ability to select their donors, as they do with other types of donation. The clinic restricts donors to those who are young enough and have no medical conditions or histories that would be of concern. Counseling is recommended for both couples in an embryo donation to make sure that everyone involved understands the process and can handle it emotionally. The FDA regulations require testing for HIV and other diseases of embryo donors, who must undergo these tests before donating embryos for use by other couples.

> **Adoption Answer**
>
> You can access a list of clinics that handle embryo donation at:
>
> **www.resolve.org**

Embryo Adoption

Another option is an *embryo adoption*, which is a modified form of embryo donation. This process is very similar to a traditional adoption and is treated as such by everyone involved. An outside agency that is not associated with the clinic that holds the frozen embryos handles the matching process. Recipients are provided with more information about the donors, just as in a traditional adoption. Counseling and home studies are performed in much the same way they would be in a traditional adoption.

Donors have some say in choosing the recipient and also have the option of staying in touch with them and possibly knowing their genetic children at some point down the line.

Legal Effect

When a woman gives birth to a child, she is legally that child's mother. If she is married, her husband is the child's legal father. This is regard-less of DNA or how the pregnancy was initiated. This overlying rule means that you do not need to go through any legal proceeding to be the legal parent of a child you gave birth to through embryo donation. If the woman has a partner she is not married to, he or she can adopt the child through a second-parent adoption and become a legal parent. California, Connecticut, Florida, Louisiana, Maryland,

Adoption Answer

Snowflakes is one of the only agencies that handles embryo adoptions in a process similar to traditional adoptions. They can be contacted at:

Snowflakes Nightlight Christian Adoptions
801 East Chapman Ave.
Suite 106
Fullerton, CA 92831
714-278-1020
www.snowflakes.org

For embryo donation information, you can contact Reprotech at:

www.reprot.com

Massachusetts, New Jersey, North Dakota, Ohio, Oklahoma, Texas, and Virginia have specific laws permitting embryo donation that make the recipient or recipient couple the legal parent or parents, or that at least require a physician to offer embryo donation as an option to couples undergoing fertility treatments. Florida permits reasonable compensation to the donors.

Other states do not have laws about embryo adoption or donation. The process is handled by a contract created by the parties. While the recipient mother or couple is/are the legal parent(s) of a child born through embryo donation or adoption, an agreement is always necessary so that everyone in the situation has complete legal protection. The couple donating the embryo, or placing it for adoption, must waive all rights to the embryo and the future child it may become. The receiving couple must waive any rights to seek child support or damages from the donating couple. Some couples that accept embryo donations are not comfortable with the lack of law in this area and thus seek to thoroughly protect themselves by going through an adoption procedure after the child is born, because if DNA tests were ever done, it would prove the child to be the product of the biological donors. It is important to talk to your attorney about how you can best protect your family and follow your state's laws.

Costs

Costs for embryo donation are less than those involved in an adoption. Costs average $2,500 to $4,000 per transfer. If your embryo is being shipped to you, you will have additional shipping costs, which run in the hundreds since the embryo must be carefully preserved during the shipping process. The donor couple is not paid for the donation.

It is important to note, however, that because the success rates are so low, you may have to do several cycles (assuming there are more embryos available), significantly adding to your costs. And even if you do several cycles, you still are not guaranteed a child as you are in traditional adoption where, sooner or later, a child will be placed with you.

> **Adoption Answer**
>
> To locate a clinic that will handle an embryo donation, ask your OB/GYN for a referral, or contact the American Society for Reproductive Medicine at **www.asrm.org**.

Agreement

Generally, there are two separate agreements involved in embryo donation. The donors sign an agreement giving up all rights to the frozen embryos. This could occur years before a recipient is found. Often, this is part of the original contract that the couple signs when they begin treatments at the clinic. Most agreements specify what will happen to unused or extra embryos. The recipients sign a separate agreement with the clinic agreeing to accept the embryo and dealing with the medical risk factors involved. Recipients must receive full disclosure of all risks. Donors and recipients usually have no direct contact and are not aware of each other's identity. Be sure to have a reproductive law attorney read any contract from a clinic before you sign it.

The agreement should contain the following:
- a complete release of all rights by the donors;
- a clear explanation of costs;
- a description of what happens if an embryo does not thaw and cannot be implanted;
- an indication that you have received full disclosure and understand the risks involved;
- an agreement as to whether or not you will receive additional donations should they be needed; and,
- a treatment program you will be receiving.

If you are interested in an embryo donation in which the donors are involved in the selection process (embryo adoption), you will find that there are no laws governing this process. Agencies that take this approach treat the process as a traditional adoption and have the donor and recipient sign consent forms as they would in a regular adoption. A home study is done. There is no legal court process involved, though, since there is no child to adopt at that point. The embryos are then transferred and implanted. In an embryo adoption situation, the donors and recipients may have agreements in place that detail what kind of contact they will have with each other after the child is born. Some people want to maintain contact, and have an open adoption situation. Others choose not to.

Embryo Donation Clinic Evaluation Questionnaire

Name of Clinic _____

Name of Contact Person _____

Date of Interview _____

Questions:

❑ What kind of release have the donors signed?

❑ Do they relinquish all rights to the embryos?

❑ How many embryos are available from this couple?

❑ Do you ever recommend using a mixture of embryos from different couples?

❑ Are there requirements and qualifications we must meet to be eligible for an embryo donation?

❑ Will I learn the names of the donors?

❑ Will the donors learn our names?

❑ What information can I learn about the donors?

❑ What medical and family history is available?

❑ Are photographs of the donor couple available?

❑ How do you match donors and recipients?

❑ Do we have any say in how the clinic matches donors and recipients?

❑ Does the donor couple have a say in how the clinic matches donors and recipients?

❑ What is your success rate with embryo donation?

❑ How many embryo donation transfers have you performed?

❑ How long have you been performing this procedure?

❏ Have any children resulted from embryos from this couple? (*You will want to know if your child has any living siblings.*)

❏ Have embryos from this couple been donated to anyone else and will they be in the future? (*You want to be sure that no one else is receiving donations, to limit the number of siblings out there in the world for your child.*)

❏ What was the age of the donors at the time of donation? (*Younger is better.*)

❏ How long has the embryo been frozen? (*An older embryo may not be as effective as a newer one.*)

❏ What kind of treatment did the donating couple undergo?

❏ Why did they donate the embryos?

❏ Are the eggs and sperm used to create the embryo the donor couple's own or were they donations?

❏ If the eggs and sperm used to create the embryo were donations, what information is available about these donors?

❏ What screening and testing has been done of the donor couple and the donated embryos?

❏ If the embryos do not survive thawing, what financial adjustments or refunds are made? (*You want some kind of adjustment.*)

❏ What are the total fees for this process?

❏ What support services are available?

Chapter 13   SURROGACY

A *surrogate* is a woman who agrees to carry a pregnancy for another person or couple. There are two types of surrogacy—one in which the surrogate is biologically related to the child, and the other in which she has no biological connection. In *traditional surrogacy,* the surrogate's own eggs are used and are inseminated with the intended father's sperm. *Gestational surrogacy* occurs when the surrogate is implanted with an embryo created with the intended parents' genetic material or with donor eggs or sperm.

Surrogacy is a type of adoption because another woman gives birth to your child, and you must then (in most states) go through an adoption process to make the child legally part of your family. Even if the child is created using the egg and sperm of the intended parents, an adoption is still necessary because another woman gives birth to the child. For couples who are unable to conceive a child themselves, but would like to raise a child who is biologically related to at least one of them, surrogacy is an excellent option.

Surrogates can be complete strangers that you locate through an agency, or sometimes they are family members, such as a woman who agrees to carry a child for her sister.

Surrogacy used to be wildly controversial, and while there are still a wide mix of laws about it, it has become much more mainstream than it ever used to be. The Organization of Parents Through Surrogacy (OPTS) estimates there are 1,500 surrogate births in the United States each year.

Surrogacy Laws

In states that do not have laws stating otherwise, when a woman gives birth to a child, she is the legal mother of the child, even if she is not the biological mother of the child or has entered into a surrogacy contract with a couple who will be the child's parents. If the woman is married, her husband is considered to be the child's legal father. Because of this, a surrogate is the legal mother of the child, regardless of where the genetic material came from, and an adoption procedure is necessary in a surrogacy situation. When a surrogacy agreement is entered into, the surrogate's husband must be a party to the contract and must revoke his rights to the child. If the intended father is the biological father, he can obtain an *order of paternity* (in some states this can happen during the pregnancy) from a court. This gives him the legal right to have access to the child at the hospital and to take the child home without any additional legal steps. The next step that must happen is that the intended mother must adopt the child in a second-parent adoption procedure. (See Chapter 4 for more information.) A few states that do not require second-parent adoption by the intended mother include Arkansas and Florida (adoption is not required if the intended parents provided the embryo).

California is one of the few states that has a fairly well-established procedure for legalizing a surrogate birth. The intended parents file a court case during the pregnancy. The surrogate and her husband consent to the surrogacy in the case. The court issues a judgment that the intended parents are the legal parents. The intended parents then can inform the hospital of this and the birth certificate will be issued

> ### Adoption Answer
> For information and support about surrogacy, contact the Organization of Parents Through Surrogacy (OPTS) at **www.opts.com** or the American Surrogacy Center at **www.surrogacy.com**.

to them. They have the right to select the child's name. However, if the surrogate provides the egg, she cannot relinquish her rights until the child is born (as in an adoption proceeding). In this case, the intended father can bring a paternity case during the pregnancy. Then the surrogate and her husband consent and the intended father is the legal father. The intended mother must use the second-parent adoption procedure to legalize her role after the birth of the child, when the surrogate can give consent to the adoption. States deal with surrogacy agreements in a widely different manner. The best thing to do is talk with a reproductive rights attorney who can advise you about the current condition of laws in your state, as well as about which state is most favorable to surrogacy.

States where it is a crime to pay for surrogacy:
- Michigan
- New Mexico
- New York
- Washington

States where surrogacy contracts are unenforceable:
- District of Columbia
- Indiana
- Louisiana
- Nebraska
- New York
- North Dakota

States with laws that specifically recognize surrogacy agreements:
- Arkansas
- Florida
- Illinois
- New Hampshire
- Nevada
- Tennessee
- Texas
- Utah
- Virginia
- Washington

States with case law about surrogacy:
- California
- Kentucky
- Massachusetts
- Ohio
- Oklahoma

California and Illinois have specific legal processes set up that give legal rights to both intended parents before the child is born. These states are considered the safest places to enter into surrogacy agreements, since they are so closely protected by state law.

California Procedure

California has a well-established procedure for legalizing surrogate birth, and because of this, California has really become the surrogacy capital of the United States. Many people go to California to find surrogates and enter into surrogacy contracts in that state because the laws are so clear and welcoming. Once the surrogate is pregnant, the intended parents first file a court case. The surrogate and her husband consent to the surrogacy in the court. The court then issues a judgment that the intended parent or parents are the legal parents. The intended parents then can inform the hospital of this and the birth certificate will be issued to them, and they have the right to select the child's name. All the legal steps are taken care of before the baby is even born, which can ease a lot of worries.

However, if the surrogate provides the egg, she cannot relinquish her rights until the child is born (as in an adoption proceeding). In this case, the intended father can bring a paternity case during the pregnancy. The surrogate and her husband consent and he is the legal father, but the ruling cannot be finalized until after the birth. If the father has a partner, he must use the second-parent adoption procedure to legalize his role.

Illinois Procedure

Illinois passed the *Surrogacy Law of 2005*, which allows intended parents to have their rights recognized before the child is born. There must be a contract for the surrogacy and a statement from a physician about the intended parents' inability to have a child on their own. The surrogate must have already given birth to one child, be at least 21 years old, undergo counseling, and have an attorney. The medical procedure must be performed in Illinois.

Surrogacy Programs

Many couples locate a surrogate through a surrogacy program managed through a fertility clinic. Adoption agencies also often coordinate surrogacy programs. These programs locate potential surrogates, prescreen them, and match them with parents. The process is very similar to that used in traditional adoption. However, because you are being matched with a woman before she is pregnant, you will have a long and ongoing relationship with her through the period leading up to conception and then through the pregnancy. It is a much more collaborative effort than an adoption. The ideal surrogate is married and has children of her own—this is because she is presumed to be mature and in a stable relationship. Being married means she has support from her husband and also has someone to financially support her during pregnancy. It also means that, presumably, most of her emotional needs are being met and she will not look to the baby to fulfill them. Having children is important because it means she understands what it is like to be pregnant and give birth. It is supposedly easier for her to carry this child for someone else and walk away if she has a real understanding of what pregnancy and birth are like and really knows the kinds of emotions she may feel after giving birth.

A woman who has never had children may be surprised at how strongly she feels about the baby when it is born and may be unable to give up the child. The thinking is that a surrogate who is a parent has been through it all and enters the agreement with experience. This does not mean that a married surrogate with children of her own will not change her mind—but it does tend to improve the odds. Adoption agencies that have surrogacy programs treat the entire process in the same way they would a regular adoption and require home studies, counseling, and communication between the parties.

It is important to choose a surrogacy program that you feel comfortable with and confident in. Once you find a potential surrogate, it is necessary that she undergo physical and psychological exams before any contract is entered into. The surrogate will also want to get to know you and decide if she feels comfortable with you. You, of course, will do the same with her. Since surrogacy involves a large degree of trust, it is important to use a surrogate you are completely comfortable with.

> ### Adoption Answer
> Read sample surrogacy contracts at:
>
> **www.surrogacy.com/ legals/gestcontract.html**
>
> **www.surromomsonline. com/articles/contract.htm**
>
> **www.everything surrogacy.com**

Finding a Surrogate on Your Own

Another option for surrogacy is to locate a surrogate on your own, without using a program. A sister, relative, or close friend may be willing to be a surrogate for you. Of course, in this situation, it is essential to use a reproductive law attorney who will advise you as to the laws in your state and will draw up a contract. Additionally, it is important that everyone involved in the surrogacy process obtain counseling, since this emotional situation is further compounded by the existing relationships. It is possible to locate a surrogate you do not know well on your own, but this is not recommended, since you cannot perform the same sophisticated screening and psychological evaluation an agency or clinic can.

Surrogacy Agreements

Surrogacy agreements are complicated and important documents. The most important feature of a surrogacy agreement is that it revokes all rights and responsibilities the surrogate and her husband have to the child. The intended parents are the legal parents to the child. Other important clauses include:

- the surrogate agrees to follow all medical advice, but medical decisions during the pregnancy are ultimately left up to her;
- the surrogate agrees to consider *multifetal reduction* (reducing the number of embryos in the pregnancy if there are more than two) if necessary;
- the state where the child will be born is specified;
- the intended parents take on all financial and medical responsibility for the child;
- the intended parents have the right to name the child;
- the surrogate agrees to use her own medical insurance, if she has any, to cover her care during the pregnancy and delivery; and,
- the surrogate agrees to abstain from intercourse for a period of time while conception is attempted, to ensure that the pregnancy occurs using the intended parent(s)' genetic material.

It is essential that you use an attorney experienced in surrogacy agreements. Even if you are working with an agency or surrogacy program, you should hire your own attorney to review the contract.

Some people may wonder why an agreement is so essential, particularly if they live in a state where the courts will not uphold a surrogacy agreement. Even if your courts will not enforce a surrogacy agreement, it would still be important evidence should you get into a custody battle with your surrogate. Agreements are also important because the negotiation process can help you spot and work out things that might be potential problems down the line. The agreement will spell out in clear terms what everyone is going to do and how all the issues involved will be handled. Also, when people sign their name to a contract, they will usually feel obligated to carry out what they are agreeing to, so the agreement is an important way for both you and the surrogate to commit to the surrogacy.

Payment Issues

The issue of paying surrogates is probably the most controversial part of the entire surrogacy process. Some people argue that paying a surrogate amounts to buying a baby and should be outlawed. Others feel that surrogates should be compensated for their time, physical discomfort, emotional turmoil, and extreme generosity.

The intended parents will always take on all medical expenses relating to the conception, pregnancy, and birth. In many cases, you will also be permitted to reimburse the surrogate for travel expenses, maternity clothes, loss of wages, and additional child care expenses. The laws governing this are the same as the laws governing reimbursement of expenses for a birth mother in an adoption. (See Chapter 7 for more information.)

Payment is often made through your attorney so there is a clear record that can be presented to the court as proof that all is done in a very forthright and honest manner.

Some states do permit payments to the surrogate to compensate her for time and discomfort. While payments are not permitted in other states, it is possible to give the surrogate a gift. Discuss this option with your attorney to find out what is permissible in your state. There may be rules about the value of the gift—it must really be a gift, not a form of payment. Some parents give their surrogate a special piece of jewelry or something else that has sentimental value and meaning. If you violate the law about payments, your parent-child relationship is not jeopardized; however, you may be subject to criminal penalties.

Insurance Coverage

If your surrogate has health insurance coverage, it should cover her pregnancy. Some surrogates do not wish to use their own insurance. Others are willing to do so if the intended parents pay all deductibles and co-pays. This is an important part of your agreement and should be included in your contract.

If your surrogate does not have health insurance coverage or will not be using her own coverage, you will need to pay for her medical expenses yourself or help her obtain a health insurance policy (which may mean paying for it yourself). Your insurance will not provide coverage until the birth. Even then, your insurance will provide coverage only if one parent is already a legal parent or if the child is officially placed with you as part of the adoption process. You will be responsible for paying the costs associated with the fertility procedures for the surrogate, which will result (hopefully!) in the pregnancy.

Problems with Surrogacy

Many people are leery of surrogacy agreements, having heard about high-profile cases in which surrogates changed their minds and refused to place the child with the intended parents. In some ways, the prospect of this is scarier than that of an adoption in which the birth mother changes her mind, since in surrogacy cases, the intended father is also the biological and legal father of the baby.

Perhaps the most famous case about surrogacy is the *Baby M* case from New Jersey in 1988. In that case, the court invalidated the surrogacy agreement, but placed the baby with the biological father. The intended mother was not permitted to adopt since the surrogate (who was the biological mother) did not give her consent. The court found that the surrogacy agreement was invalid because the surrogate was paid. If the agreement did not include payment, it would have been valid. Another landmark case is the *Johnson v. Calvert* case decided in California in 1993. In this case, the surrogate was implanted with a zygote that was created using genetic material from both the intended mother and intended father. The surrogate was not biologically related to the child. The court held that the legal parents are those who were intended to be the parents under the agreement. According to the court, the parent of a surrogate child is whomever is intended by the parties to be the parent, not who is biologically related to the child or who carries the pregnancy.

An Ohio case from 1994, *Belsito v. Clark,* held that unless legal waiver or consent is provided, the people who provide the genetic material for the child are the natural parents of the child. This means that if the surrogate provides the egg, she is the legal mother, but can give her consent for the adoption.

In most cases, a surrogate does not change her mind, especially when you use a respected surrogacy program that will carefully screen all potential surrogates and help you find a good match. However, should something go wrong and the surrogate change her mind, you first need to consult an attorney so that you can fully understand the laws in your state. As described earlier in this chapter, some states will not enforce surrogacy contracts.

If the intended father is the biological father of the child, at the very minimum, he will have access to the child until the case is resolved. There is a very good chance that the father will be able to obtain custody, and through him, the intended mother would be able to have time with the child. If the surrogate provided the egg, she will at the very least be entitled to have contact with the child (unless the birth is in a state where surrogacy contracts are enforced). If the surrogate did not provide the egg, the case for the intended parents is stronger, but not completely decided unless your state enforces surrogacy agreements.

The surrogate's husband would have an initial claim to the child, since any child born to a woman during marriage is legally considered to be her husband's legal child. However, DNA tests would make it clear who the real father is and the husband's claim would be denied.

If a surrogate is related to the child and she changes her mind, and your state does not uphold agreements, you are facing a situation in which the child would have to split his or her time between you and the surrogate. It is for this reason that many people are particular about the states in which they enter into surrogacy agreements.

Most surrogacy arrangements go without a hitch, so the odds are quite good that you will not experience a problem. The best thing to do though is to protect yourself as much as possible up front. Use only a reputable surrogacy agency, choose only a surrogate who has had children, and listen to your gut. Hire a good attorney who can create a solid agreement for your surrogacy.

Other Steps to Protect Yourself

As soon as you have entered into a surrogacy agreement, it is essential that you have a will drawn up or update an existing will. You will want to name a *guardian* for your child should anything happen to you. You want to have a clear legal plan for who would care for your child should you and your spouse pass away.

If you must go through a second-parent adoption process to make the intended mother the legal mother, there will likely be weeks or months until the adoption is final. In this time period, the father will have all the legal rights to make medical decisions for the child, but the intended mother will only have these rights if they are given to her in writing. The father should execute a written consent giving the mother the right to make medical decisions for the child.

Choosing a Surrogacy Program Questionnaire

Name of Agency _____

Name of Contact Person _____

Date of Interview _____

Questions:

❑ How do you recruit and locate surrogates?

❑ How do you screen potential surrogates?

❑ What medical and psychological tests are surrogates required to undergo?

❑ How do you screen the intended parents?

❑ Do you provide counseling for both surrogate and intended parents?

❑ What is your role in coordinating the surrogacy?

❑ What fees are involved?

❑ Are the fees refundable if the surrogacy is not completed?

❑ Does this differ with miscarriage as opposed to a surrogate who changes her mind?

❑ Is there a waiting list?

❑ How many potential surrogates do you have in the program?

❑ How many intended parents are you working with now?

❑ Will you work with surrogates brought in by the intended parents?

❑ What kind of relationship do you recommend that intended parents have with their surrogate?

❏ Is there any post-birth contact with your program?

❏ Have any of your surrogates changed their minds after becoming pregnant?

❏ How do you handle this situation?

❏ How many births does your program have a year?

❏ How many total births have you had? What percent result in successful placement?

❏ How long have you been doing this?

❏ Can you provide the names of parents to contact for references?

❏ Do intended parents have the right to refuse proposed surrogates?

❏ Does the surrogate have her own attorney when signing the agreement?

❏ What kind of background information do you provide about the surrogate?

❏ How do you deal with the surrogate's expenses?

❏ How are they accounted and paid for?

Chapter 14

COPING WITH ADOPTION

Adoption might be one of the bright moments in your life, but there will most likely be bumps along the road as you work through the process. Working through the difficulties, challenges, or disappointments might not be easy but will be worth it once you achieve your ultimate goal of adopting a child.

Dealing with Reactions to Adoption

While most people think of adoption as a good thing, many people still think they need to distinguish between adoptive children and biological children. "That's Mary's adopted daughter," you may hear someone say, when to you, your child is just your child. It does not matter to you how your child came into your family—that is the smallest detail in your eyes.

Parents who adopt a child who does not resemble them will often be asked by strangers if the child is adopted. Some people go on to ask for details about the adoption. Some people are bold enough to just march up and ask you outright where your child is "from." For example, if you adopt a child from Korea and you are not Asian, people may come up to you and ask what country your child is from, whether you knew his or her parents, and other details about the adoption. Each person who adopts has to make his or her own decision about how much information they are willing to share with other people about the adoption. You may feel that this kind of information is no one's business but yours and your child's. While these questions are often well-intentioned (other times they are just plain nosy), they send a message to your child that he or she is different, that there is something strange about the way he or she entered your family, and that it is something to be questioned or discussed. Some parents choose not to discuss these details with other people and instead respond by explaining that they do not wish to discuss the private details of their family with other people. Some adoptive parents simply come up with an appropriate response that closes the subject for good, such as "I don't discuss details with strangers" or "Taylor is my daughter. Period."

You may also encounter people who assume that because you adopted, you had fertility problems. This is a misconception (so to speak!), since many people choose adoption without ever attempting to get pregnant. It can be insulting for people to assume that adopting was a second choice or last-ditch effort, when in fact adopting is something you very much wanted. If you did try fertility treatments, that is likely a very private aspect of your life and one you probably do not wish to discuss with others. If people ask questions about whether you tried fertility treatments, you can ignore their questions or simply say how pleased you are to have the wonderful child you have. You can be blunt and explain it is really none of their business at all. What can be most disconcerting is the feeling that because you adopted your child, some people believe he or she is not really *yours* in the same way a biological child would be. You never hear anyone referring to someone's child as their "biological child," but you quite often hear a reference to a person's "adopted child." This is the kind of distinction many adoptive parents are working to change. Those who adopt know that it does not matter how a child comes to you. Your child is your child, and how he or she joined your family is simply not important.

Dealing with Others Involved in Your Case

Because adoptions sometimes take longer than it seems they should, it is easy to become frustrated and annoyed with the people who seem to be holding it up—or at least not moving it along as quickly as you would like. While it is sometimes necessary to ask the tough questions and find out why there are delays, it is important to remember that you need to deal with the people involved with your adoption in a polite and friendly way. While adding a child to your family is a critical event for you, these people are simply doing their jobs—as rewarding as that may be—and they do not have the same sense of urgency, impatience, and frustration that you may feel. While it is understandable that you may need to express your frustration and want solid answers about delays or problems, it is not a good idea to personally attack or argue with workers and officials. These people are the ones who are moving your case along. In general, you want to be cooperative when dealing with them and your goal should be to get them to like you if possible. Things move more quickly when there are good relations in place. Do not let your first assumption be that someone has dropped the ball or not taken care of paperwork. Instead, if you do need to inquire, do so in a friendly and polite way that is not accusatory.

When dealing with an international adoption, it can be even more frustrating to have your fate held up by people you cannot even communicate with. When doing an international adoption, it is important that you work closely with your agency and that you are able to trust them to handle things for you. Make sure that if you travel to your child's country of origin, you know how to reach your agency at all hours if there is a problem or if you need help. Simply put, when you are doing an international adoption, you must expect delay. The systems in other countries do not work in the same way as our systems do in the United States. Even when you are there to get your child, there can be unexpected and unexplained delays and problems. In these situations, you have to rely on your escorts to help you resolve the problems.

Dealing with the Waiting

Whether you are waiting through a birth mother's pregnancy, for a foreign country to match you with a child, or for a domestic agency to complete your home study, you will feel a level of anxiety and impatience. You feel as if you are so close to getting your child, but so far away at the same time.

Remind yourself that adoption is a long process. Take things one step at a time and try to enjoy a sense of progress each time you move closer to the final resolution. You are moving through the process and each day brings you closer to the day you will bring your child home.

Joining an adoption support group can give you a place to talk about your feelings, offer you the chance to hear other people's experiences, and get advice. The waiting game can be hard on your relationship as well. You and your spouse or partner may find that you are on edge or more tense than usual. This too is normal. Remember that you are in this together and have the same ultimate goal. An adoption support group can help you cope with these feelings. You will not feel so alone once you meet other people who have gone through or are going through the same experiences and feelings that you are.

Dealing with Doubts

Adoption is a life-changing event. It is normal to experience doubts or have questions about the entire decision or process. The best way to deal with doubts or questions is head-on. Look closely at your concerns. If you are doubting your ability to care for or love your adoptive child, you can rest assured that there will not be a problem once that child comes home to you. Counseling can be a big help in getting you to identify things you are worried or uncomfortable about and providing an outlet for you to work through the issues. Your adoption agency may be able to suggest a counselor experienced in working with adoptive parents.

If you are worried about parenting skills, consider taking a parenting class. Doubts about the agency, birth mother, or social worker should be carefully considered. Express your concerns to the agency or to your attorney. Try to talk through these concerns and obtain reassurances to ease your mind. That being said, there are times when you just know something is wrong or not working. In those instances, you should listen to your gut feelings.

Changing Your Mind

You can change your mind about the adoption any time until it is finalized. You may still be liable for expenses and fees up to that point. If you have serious unresolved doubts about the adoption or your situation has changed so that adoption is no longer a good decision for you, it is better to confront them now before you become an adoptive child's parent. The child you were going to adopt will be placed elsewhere, so you need not feel guilty.

Some families are lucky enough to unexpectedly become pregnant while attempting to adopt a child. The pregnancy does not affect your ability to adopt, unless *you* decide that it does. There is nothing wrong with continuing the adoption while you are pregnant, or with deciding not to complete the adoption if that is what will work best for your family.

Taking Time Off for Your Adoption

You should check with your employer to determine if they offer paid or unpaid time off to complete an adoption. Some employers have special provisions for this in order to encourage and support adoption.

Check with your human resources contact for information on benefits for adoptions. Depending on your company's policy, you may also qualify for a maternity/paternity leave. You can also plan to take time off once the adoption is complete under the federal *Family and Medical Leave Act* (FMLA) or your state family leave law (check with your human resources department to determine if your state has such a law). You are eligible for a federal FMLA leave if you work for a public agency (federal, state, or local) or for a private employer with fifty or more employees and have been employed there at least twelve months and worked at least 1,250 hours in the last twelve months. You can take up to twelve weeks of unpaid leave and you can take this time all together or break it up, or even use it to return to work part-time after the adoption. When possible, you must provide your employer with thirty days' notice, but in some adoption cases this is not possible, so just provide whatever notice you can.

> **Adoption Answer**
>
> If you experience any problems with your FMLA request, contact the Department of Labor at:
>
> **www.dol.gov**

> **Adoption Answer**
>
> Read about adoption attachment and bonding issues at:
>
> **http://attachment. adoption.com**

Under FMLA, your employer must keep your health benefits in place (but you may have to pay premiums while you are out) and must restore you to your original job or to an equivalent job with equivalent pay when you return. Your employer cannot penalize you for taking the leave or allow it to affect any of your benefits. If you return to work and your employer has taken away some of your job responsibilities or cut your hours, this would be a violation.

If you and your spouse work for the same employer, you are entitled to a total of twelve weeks unpaid FMLA leave divided between both of you in a twelve-month period to care for your child. So, for example, you could take ten weeks and your spouse could take two weeks. Your leaves can be taken simultaneously. Spouses who work for different employers are entitled to each take the full FMLA twelve weeks.

Bonding with an Adopted Child

Many adoptive parents are worried about how well they will bond with their child. When a child becomes part of your life, your heart will open to make room for him or her. There is often the expectation that bonding is immediate—that once you see or hold your child you will immediately fall in love with him or her. Sometimes bonding is a gradual process, so do not be disappointed or upset if it takes you a little while to adjust to the new person in your life. If this is something you are very concerned about, talk with other adoptive parents to learn how their feelings grew for their child.

Dealing with Adoption Disappointments

Occasionally adoption disappointments happen—a birth mother might decide not to place her newborn, a child that has been selected for you might have needs you feel you cannot meet, or something else may go wrong during the process to keep an adoption from happening. Birth mothers have the right to change their minds after the birth, so no adoption is certain until the court has made it legal. If you do experience a disappointment like this, it is important to give yourself time and space to deal with it. A particular dream that you had has ended. Some potential adoptive parents decide that they cannot try to adopt again after a disappointment, but most do try again. You might need some time to heal, or you might be able to move forward immediately to find a new child or birth mother.

Adoption support groups can be a lifesaver when you are confronted with a disappointment, so seek one out if you need support or advice. If a child has been placed with you, but the adoption has been cancelled, you might consider seeing a counselor who can help with the deep feelings of loss associated with this kind of situation.

> **Adoption Answer**
>
> Support and assistance with failed adoptions is available at:
>
> **http://forums. adoption.com/ failed-contested- adoption**

Chapter 15

RAISING AN ADOPTED CHILD

Once an adoption is complete, you can move on with the joy of being a family and raising your new child. However, raising an adopted child is not always the same as raising a biological child and there are some concerns and issues that may arise.

Celebrating Your Adoption

Once your adoption is complete, you will probably want to introduce your new family member to friends and family. Some people choose to send adoption announcements or hold a celebration or ceremony to welcome the child into the family. Many families treat an adoption as they would any other birth, with a baby shower.

As your child grows, you will need to think about how you will recognize the adoption. Some families hang special plaques in their home to commemorate an adoption. Other families celebrate their child's adoption day each year with a special celebration. Each family must make its own decisions about what they are comfortable with and what is the best way to mark this important event.

Worrying about Your Adoption

Some parents find themselves worrying after an adoption has occurred that something will happen to take their child away from them. You should only be concerned if the laws were not followed in your case, or you knowingly did something illegal. If this is not the case (and it almost never is), you can rest assured that your child belongs to you and you alone, and no one is ever going to interfere with that. Your adoption cannot be "undone" or reversed. Even if a birth mother did change her mind, as long as she signed all consents and it was done by the books, the adoption is completely and totally final. You have absolutely nothing to worry about.

Breastfeeding an Adopted Infant

You may be surprised to learn that it is possible to breastfeed an adopted infant. Some mothers choose to breastfeed an adopted infant because of the known health benefits of breastfeeding or as a way to bond with the child, provide comfort, and create a physical connection to a child that you are not biologically connected to. For some women, it just feels natural to want to feed and nurture your child yourself.

> **Adoption Answer**
>
> For more information about how to breastfeed an adopted child, see:
>
> **www.breastfeeding. adoption.com**
>
> **www.lalecheleague.org/ NB/NBadoptive.html**

The stimulation of nursing will cause a rise in prolactin, a hormone that stimulates milk production. However, adoptive mothers usually cannot produce enough milk on their own. Lactation aids can be used, providing supplementary formula to the infant while breastfeeding. Contact your pediatrician's office and ask to meet with a lactation consultant on staff. If your doctor is not supportive, find one who is.

Talking to Your Existing Children about Adoption

If you have existing children, the adoption of a new brother or sister will be a time of excitement, as well as anxiety. Many of the concerns and problems that arise are the same as those that occur when a child is added to the family through biological means. You are adding another child who will infringe on the time and attention the existing children receive. However, there are some concerns that are unique to the adoption situation. Young children in the family may be terrified at the thought of a parent placing a child for adoption and may fear that this will happen to them. You will need to reassure your child that you are not placing any of your children for adoption and that this happens only in very unique circumstances. Explaining the situation of how this new child came to be placed for adoption can help ease their fears.

Some people are surprised to learn that children tend to be very accepting of children who come from other cultures or who appear physically different. It is likely that if this is not an issue for you, that it will not be for your existing children. Some adoptive parents have funny stories to tell, such as existing children wondering when the newly adopted child will be sent back. Your children's questions and comments are innocent, but always deserve serious answers.

If you have an existing child who joined your family through adoption, the adoption of another child is still likely to be an event that causes some anxiety. Even though your child knows he or she was adopted, the thought of adding another child to the family can be difficult. You should not expect the adjustment period to be any easier or smoother simply because your existing child was adopted as well.

Depending on the age of your existing children, there are different ways to discuss adoption. Getting a book about adoption can be one good way to explain it to your child. Another idea is to talk to your child about all the things parents do for their children—putting them to bed, changing diapers, feeding them, loving them, and so on. Then explain to your child that another thing parents do is bring the child into the world. Explain that children who are adopted have one set of parents who bring them into the world, but are unable to do all the other things a parent has to do, so the child gets adoptive parents who will do everything else for them for the rest of their lives. This will help prevent a biological child from worrying that you will one day not want him or her and place him or her for adoption.

It is important to make sure your child does not think of an adoptive child as one who was not wanted. Focus the discussion on the birth parents not being able to care for the child or give him or her everything he or she needs. If you refer to the adopted child as unwanted, you are setting the stage for a biological child to taunt your adoptive child.

> **Adoption Answer**
>
> For more information on breastfeeding for adoptive parents, see the Adoptive Breastfeeding Resource website at:
>
> **www.fourfriends.com/ abrw**

Existing children may resent the attention an adopted child receives, especially if the new child has special needs or a situation that requires a lot of time and energy from the parents. It always takes work to help everyone adjust when you add a child to the family. Adoption situations are no different. Time, patience, and understanding are often the best remedies. Sometimes, family counseling can help everyone in the family adjust to the situation.

Raising Biological and Adopted Siblings

If you are raising a family created through birth and adoption, there is sure to be conflict—but there is conflict any time you have siblings, whether they are biologically related or not. It is essential you treat all of your children fairly and with respect and that they understand they are all equal parts of the family. It is also important to emphasize to children that all people are different and family members are different too. Your differences are what make your family special. Children take their cues from the parents. If you feel your adopted child is a full member of your family, they will as well.

If you are raising a child of a different ethnicity or from a different culture, you may wish to educate your adoptive child and existing children (as well as yourself) about the history, culture, and traditions of the country or group of people. Doing so gives your adopted child a sense of identity, involves your family in his or her past, and shows that you celebrate and appreciate who your child is and where he or she came from. You may also wish to spend time with families that have adopted children with similar backgrounds. (See Appendix A for a list of such organizations.)

Talking to Your Adoptive Child about the Adoption

Many parents tell their adoptive child basic information about his or her adoption from the very beginning. The story of how the child joined the family becomes a treasured one that is told over and over. When talking about adoption, most experts recommend that you emphasize that the birth mother or father made the placement decision out of love and concern. Some adoptive parents choose to emphasize that the child was meant to be part of this family, while de-emphasizing the idea that another family or mother did not want the child.

It is also helpful to point out to your children that families are made in many ways—through birth, stepparenting, surrogacy, foster care, and so on. How the family was created is unimportant, but the fact that it exists is the primary fact. When you talk to your child about adoption, be sure to share how you felt and how important the adoption was to you and the entire family. Share details of the adoption, just as you would share details of a biological child's birth.

As your child grows older, you may be able to share more details about the adoption, such as the birth mother's name or facts about her. Being open with your child about the facts will help him or her feel comfortable with his or her own personal history. As children become older, they want and need more details and often want to know specifics about their birth parents. As an adoptive parent, your role is to supply what information you can and offer support. If you have remained in contact with the birth parent, you will have a lot you can share. If you have no identifying information about the birth parents, your child can register with various adoptee groups to attempt to make contact with the birth parents. (See Appendix A for more information.) The amount of information you share with your child at various points in his or her life will be up to you. In large part, you should take your cues from your child. Offer age-appropriate information when he or she is interested in learning more.

> **Adoption Answer**
>
> For more information about talking to your child about adoption, see:
>
> **www.adopting.org/ talk.html**
>
> **www.rainbowkids.com**

Keeping an Adoption a Secret

It is possible to keep an adoption a secret—after all, this is how adoptions used to be done. For the most part, it is not thought by experts to be a good idea anymore. Adopted children who are raised as if they are biological children may find out at some point that they were adopted. They certainly will wonder why they look different from the rest of the family, and as they get older, not having basic information about their genetic parents can cause problems for medical care.

Discovering that you were adopted and it was kept a secret can be very hurtful and disappointing. Think carefully about your reasons for wanting to keep the adoption a secret and how it can benefit your family. Weigh this against your child's need to know his or her own history and the sense of betrayal that is possible should the information ever be revealed. Ultimately the choice is yours, and you should parent as you see best.

Cultural Heritage

If your child has a cultural or ethnic heritage different from your own, you will want to share your own history and traditions with him or her. You may also want to try to incorporate some of his or her background into your family. Some adoptive parents who adopt internationally take many photos when they visit their child's country so they can later show him or her what it is like. Buying books and traditional clothing and games from your child's country is another way to help him or her connect with the past. Learn about the holidays and traditions from your child's country or ethnic group and celebrate them.

> ### Adoption Answer
> Consider joining an adoption support group for parents of children from specific countries, such as Families with Children From China at:
>
> **www.fwcc.org**
>
> or Families with Children from Viet Nam at:
>
> **www.fcvn.org**

Your heritage will be important to your child as well and will become part of his or her own heritage. Your child will grow up eating your family's foods and celebrating your holidays. These things will belong to him or her just as they belong to you. However, some adoptive children may at some point feel as if participating in these things is somehow false for them. With a little encouragement and enthusiasm, you can let your child know that he or she is a very real part of your cultural line.

Medical Issues

When you adopt your child, you will receive some kind of medical history for him or her. This will include information about his or her health and may include a family history if available. It is important to obtain as much information as you can. This may mean asking several times or paying for translations of documents from another language if your adoption is an international one. The more information you are able to gather, the better. While your child may come to you in good health, he or she will need a detailed history later in life and any information you can obtain will be helpful. Some children come to adoption with very little medical history. Do not be concerned. Your child still has every chance to grow up to be healthy. Get as much information as you can and realize that whatever you can obtain will have to be enough.

Post-Adoption Support

Adoption support groups are great ways to get information and support while you are in the adoption process, but they are also important in the post-adoption period. A support group can help you and your child through the adjustments you face right after an adoption, as well as with the ongoing issues that pop up from time to time in an adopted child's life. It can be so wonderful to know there are people you can turn to who are going through or who have gone through exactly what you are. Children can connect with other adopted children through these groups. Also, once you have gone through an adoption, you are in the perfect position to offer help and encouragement to potential adoptive parents who contact the group for information. (See Appendix A for information on support groups.)

Finding Birth Parents

As your child matures, he or she may wish to learn more about his or her birth parents, country of origin, or background. Some parents keep scrapbooks for their adopted children that include the birth mother letter they wrote, photos they took in the child's country of origin, photos of birth parents, adoption paperwork, or letters from birth parents. Depending on the type of adoption, finding your child's birth parent can vary in difficulty.

Start with the agency you worked with and contact information you had at the time of adoption. You should also check *mutual consent registries*, where parties to an adoption can register and agree to be contacted if the other party should access the registry. Even if your child's parent is not registered there, your child can register in the hopes of the birth parent one day contacting the registry. Twenty-nine states have established these registries. In those states, your child needs a court order to access his or her original birth certificate, if you do not have a copy. You may need to hire an investigator to eventually find the birth parents.

Glossary

A

adoptee. Person being adopted.

adoption. A process in which a child becomes part of another family through legal means.

adoption agency. An organization that arranges adoptions.

adoption assistance agreement. A contract between adoptive parents and the state agency that placed the child, describing the monthly payments the state will make to the parents to help with the expense of raising a child.

adult adoption. Adoption by one adult of another adult.

agency adoption. An adoption in which an agency connects the birth mother and intended parents and handles the mechanics and paperwork.

American Association of Tissue Banks (AATB). A voluntary organization that accredits sperm and egg donation banks.

B

background check. An investigation into a person's criminal history.

biological parent. A person who provided genetic material to create a child.

birth father. The biological father of the child.

birth mother. The biological mother of the child. Also sometimes defined as the woman who physically gave birth to the child.

birth parent. The biological parent of the child.

C

Child Citizenship Act of 2000. A federal law that allows an internationally adopted child to automatically become a U.S. citizen.

closed adoption. An adoption whereby the child has no information about the birth parents.

consent. A legal agreement that an adoption should take place.

consulate. A government's office in another country, through which it can assist citizens visiting the foreign country.

cryopreservation. The freezing of eggs, sperm, or embryos.

D

domestic adoption. An adoption of a child born in the United States.

donor. A person who donates egg, sperm, or embryo for another to use.

E

embassy. An official headquarters of a government inside a foreign country.

embryo. An egg fertilized with sperm that has begun to divide.

embryo adoption. A process in which an embryo is donated to another couple or person and adoption-type procedures are followed, such as home studies and possible contact between the parties.

embryo donation. A donation to another couple or for use in research of an embryo created during fertility treatments.

F

facilitator. A professional who arranges adoptions.

Family and Medical Leave Act (FMLA). A federal law that allows up to twelve weeks of unpaid time off from work when you are dealing with your own medical conditions (such as fertility treatments) or caring for a family member, such as a newborn or adopted child.

foster care. A situation in which a child who is in the custody of the state is temporarily cared for by adults licensed by the state.

foster parent. An adult who contracts with an agency to care for children who are in the custody of the state.

G

gestational surrogacy. The intended mother's egg is implanted into the surrogate with the intended father's sperm to conceive a child. The surrogate has no biological relationship with the child.

guardianship. A legal proceeding giving someone the authority to make decisions for another person, usually a child or a person who is mentally incompetent.

H

Health Insurance Portability and Accountability Act (HIPAA). A federal law that makes medical records confidential.

home study. A process through which a licensed social worker meets with prospective adoptive parents and evaluates their lifestyle and home for its appropriateness to house a child.

I

Immigration and Naturalization Service (INS). The previous name of the department whose duties are now administered by the USCIS.

independent adoption. An adoption in which the adoptive parent locates the child or birth mother instead of having an agency do so.

Indian Child Welfare Act. A federal law specifying that a Native American child must be placed with relatives, within the tribe, or with other Native Americans before other options are considered.

international adoption. An adoption of a child born in another country.

K

kinship adoption. An adoption of a child who is a relative.

kinship agreement. An agreement outlining contact that birth parents and other relatives will have with a child who has been adopted.

L

legal parent. A parent who is considered to be a child's parent in the eyes of the law.

legal risk placement. A placement of a foster care child with potential adoptive parents. The adoption is not finalized because the child may need to be reunited with his or her parents, should a court make that decision.

M

minor. A child under the age of 18.

Multiethnic Placement Act. A federal law that denies funding to adoption agencies that delay or deny placement because of race.

N

notice. A legal notification of an adoption proceeding.

O

open adoption. An adoption in which the child is aware that he or she was adopted and one in which he or she may or may not have contact with the birth parents.

ovum. Egg cell, female reproductive cell.

P

parent-initiated adoption. An adoption in which the adoptive parent locates the child or birth mother instead of having an agency do so.

petition. A legal document asking a court to approve an adoption.

post-adoption agreement. See kinship agreement.

private adoption. An adoption that does not involve an agency. The birth mother and intended parents work directly with each other.

putative father registry. A state registry that allows a man to record the fact that he believes he is the father of the child, before the child is born.

R

readoption. Legal process in which parents of a child adopted internationally go through a U.S. adoption.

revocation. Legally taking back consent for an adoption.

S

second-parent adoption. An adoption of a child by his or her stepparent.

social worker. A professional who performs home studies and assists families with adjustments to adoptions.

special needs child. A child who has a physical or mental disability.

standby guardianship. A type of guardianship in which a terminally ill parent names a guardian who is able to immediately become a child's guardian upon the parent's death.

stepchild. The child of a spouse from a previous relationship.

stepparent. The person married to a child's mother or father, who is not his or her legal parent.

success rate. The percent or successful pregnancies a clinic produces.

surrogacy. The process by which a surrogate carries a pregnancy for the intended parent(s) and has no legal ties to the child.

surrogacy agreement. A contract made with a surrogate in which she agrees to carry the couple's child and which allows them to become the child's legal parents. It often includes provisions for the intended parents to pay her expenses through the pregnancy.

surrogate. A woman who carries a pregnancy for the intended parent(s) without any legal ties to the child. She may or may not provide the egg cell needed for the pregnancy.

T

traditional surrogacy. The surrogate's own eggs are used in conjunction with sperm from the intended father to conceive a child. The surrogate is biologically related to the resulting child.

U

United States Citizenship and Immigration Services (USCIS). A division of the Department of Homeland Security, which regulates immigration.

V

visa. An immigration document that allows a person to enter a country.

W

will. A legal document that disposes of a person's assets after his or her death. It can also include a provision for guardianship of a child.

Appendix A: Resources

This appendix provides numerous additional resources as you go through the process of building a family and dealing with the issues these decisions bring. In it you will find information on books, both for adults and children, organizations, and websites all designed to help your process be more informed and supported.

Books for Adults

Adopting After Infertility
by Patricia Irwin Johnston

Adoption Is a Family Affair!
  What Relatives and
  Friends Must Know
by Patricia Irwin Johnston

Adopting On Your Own:
  The Complete Guide to
  Adoption for Single Parents
by Lee Varon

Adoption Lifebook:
A Bridge to Your Child's Beginnings
by Cindy Probst

Adoption Parenting: Creating a
  Toolbox, Building Connections
by Jean MacLeod

Attaching in Adoption:
  Practical Tools for Today's Parents
by Deborah D. Gray

Breastfeeding the Adopted Baby
by Debra Stewart Peterson

Cross Cultural Adoption: How to
  Answer Questions from
  Family, Friends, and Community
by Amy Coughlin and
  Caryn Abramowitz

Gay & Lesbian Parenting Choices:
  From Adopting or Using a Surrogate
  to Choosing the Perfect Father
by Brette Sember

A Guide to Foster Parenting:
  Everything But the Kids!
by Mary Ann Goodearle, MS

How to Adopt Internationally:
  A Guide for Agency-Directed and
  Independent Adoptions
by Jean Nelson-Erichsen and
  Heino R. Erichsen

Is Adoption for You?
  The Information You Need to Make
  the Right Choice
by Christine Adamec

Launching a Baby's Adoption:
  Practical Strategies for
  Parents and Professionals
by Patricia Irwin Johnston

Open Adoption Experience:
  Complete Guide for Adoptive and
  Birth Families
by Lois Ruskai Melina

Parenting Your Adopted Child
by Christine Adamec

Practical Tools for Foster Parents
by Lana Temple-Plotz

Pathways to Parenthood:
  The Ultimate Guide to Surrogacy
by Stacy Ziegler

The Post-Adoption Blues:
  Overcoming the Unforseen
  Challenges of Adoption
by Karen J. Foli

Single Mothers by Choice:
  A Guidebook for Single Women
  Who Are Considering or Have
  Chosen Motherhood
by Jane Mattes

Surrogate Motherhood:
  Conception in the Heart
by Helena Ragoné

Toddler Adoption:
  The Weaver's Craft
by Mary Hopkins-Best

Twenty Things Adopted Kids Wish
  Their Adoptive Parents Knew
by Sherrie Eldridge

Books for Children

Adoption Is for Always
by Linda Walvoord Girard

The Best Single Mom in the World:
  How I Was Adopted
by Mary Zisk

The Day We Met You
by Phoebe Koehler

Did My First Mother Love Me?
  A Story for an Adopted Child
by Kathryn Ann Miller and
  Jami Moffett

Filling in the Blanks:
  A Guided Look at Growing Up
  Adopted
by Susan Gabel

Happy Adoption Day!
by John McCutcheon

Heart of Mine: A Story of Adoption
by Dan Hojer

How I Was Adopted
by Joanna Cole and Maxie Chambliss

I Love You Like Crazy Cakes
by Rose A. Lewis and Jane Dyer

Let's Talk About It: Adoption
by Fred Rogers

Mommy Far, Mommy Near:
  An Adoption Story
by Carol Antoinette Peacock and
  Shawn Costello Brownell

My Special Family: A Children's Book
  About Open Adoption
by Kathleen Silber and
  Debra Marks Parelskin

Never Never Never Will She
  Stop Loving You
by Jolene Durrant and Steve Allred

Over the Moon: An Adoption Tale
by Karen Katz

Rosie's Family: An Adoption Story
by Lori Rosove and Heather Burrill

Seeds of Love:
  For Brothers and Sisters of
  International Adoption
by Mary Ebejer Petertyl and
  Jill Chambers

Two Birthdays for Beth
by Gay Lynn Cronin and
  Joanne Bowring

We Wanted You
by Liz Rosenberg and
  Peter Catalanotto

When You Were Born in China:
  A Memory Book for Children
  Adopted from China
by Sara Dorow and Stephen Wunrow

When You Were Born in Korea:
  A Memory Book for Children
  Adopted from Korea
by Brian E. Boyd

Where Are My Birth Parents?
  A Guide for Teenage Adoptees
by Karen Gravelle and Susan Fischer

Who Am I?
  And Other Questions of Adopted
  Kids (Plugged in)
by Charlene C. Giannetti

Why Was I Adopted?
by Carole Livingston

Magazines

Adoption Today Magazine
541 East Garden Drive, Unit N
Windsor, CO 80550
888-924-6736
www.adoptinfo.net

Adoptive Families Magazine
42 West 38th Street
Suite 901
New York, NY 10018
646-366-0830
www.adoptivefamilies.com

Adopting for Tomorrow
5165 West Woodmill Drive
Suite 12
Wilmington, DE 19808
888-281-1284
www.adoptingtomorrow.com

Organizations

American Academy of Adoption Attorneys
P.O. Box 33053
Washington, DC 20033
202-832-2222
www.adoptionattorneys.org

*Association of Administrators of the
  Interstate Compact on
  Adoption and Medical Assistance*
810 First Street, NE
Suite 500
Washington, DC 20002
202-682-0100
http://aaicama.aphsa.org

*Child Welfare Information Gateway
  Children's Bureau/ACYF*
1250 Maryland Avenue, SW
Eighth Floor
Washington, DC 20024
888-394-3366
703-385-7565
www.childwelfare.gov

Families for Private Adoption
P.O. Box 6375
Washington, DC 20015-0375
202-722-0338
www.ffpa.org

Family Pride Coalition
P.O. Box 65327
Washington, DC 20035
202-331-5015
www.familypride.org

Generations United
1333 H Street, NW
Suite 500 W
Washington, DC 20005
202-289-3979
www.gu.org

Grandparents as Parents
P.O. Box 964
Lakewood, CA 90714
310-924-3996

*Joint Council on International
  Children's Services*
117 South Saint Asaph Street
Alexandria, VA 22314
703-535-8045
www.jcics.org

*National Adoption Assistance Training
  Resource and Information Network*
970 Raymond Avenue
Suite 106
St. Paul, MN 55114
800–470–6665

National Adoption Foundation
100 Mill Plain Road
Danbury, CT 06811
203-791-3811
www.nafadopt.org

National Council for Adoption
225 North Washington Street
Alexandria, VA 22314
703-299-6633
www.adoptioncouncil.org

*National Council for Single
  Adoptive Parents*
P.O. Box 15084
Chevy Chase, MD 20825
*National Child Welfare Resource
  Center for Adoption*
16250 Northland Drive
Suite 120
Southfield, MI 48075
248–443–0306
www.nrcadoption.org

*North American Council on
  Adoptable Children*
970 Raymond Avenue
Suite 106
St. Paul, MN 55114
651-644-3036
www.nacac.org

Websites

Adoption Groups
www.adoptiongroups.com

Adoption Laws
www.law.cornell.edu/topics/
  adoption.html

Self-Assessment Adoption Quiz
http://adopting.adoption.com/child/
  self-assessment-adoption-quiz.html

*Adoptive Families Magazine
  Support Group Database*
www.adoptivefamilies.com/
  support_group

*American Association of
  Open Adoption Agencies*
www.openadoption.org

Association of Multiethnic Americans
www.ameasite.org

Children of Lesbians and Gays Everywhere
www.colage.org

Child Welfare League of America
www.cwla.org

Choosing an Adoption Agency
www.adoptivefamilies.com/
  articles.php?aid=308

Comeunity Adoption Support
www.comeunity.com

Domestic versus International Adoption
www.adoptall.com/intguide.html

Families with Children from China
www.fwcc.org

Families with Children from Viet Nam
www.fcvn.org

Foster Care Adoption
www.DaveThomasFoundationfor
  Adoption.org

*Gay and Lesbian-Friendly
  Adoption Agencies*
www.hrc.org

Home Study Sample
www.1–800-homestudy.com/
  homestudy/sample

How to Make Adoption Affordable
www.nefe.org/adoption
*Joint Council of International
  Children's Services*
www.jcics.org

La Leche League
www.laleche.org

Medicaid Information
www.cms.hhs.gov/medicaid

Child Welfare Information Gateway
(division of the U.S. Department of
  Health and Human Services)
www.childwelfare.org

*National Dissemination Center for
  Children with Disabilities*
www.nichcy.org

Older Child Adoption
www.olderchildadoption.com

Open Adoption Resources
www.r2press.com

Single Parent Adoption Network
http://members.aol.com/
  Onemomfor2

State Public Adoption Agencies
www.childwelfare.gov/nad

U.S. Adoption Laws by State
www.abcadoptions.com/uslaw.htm

U.S. Department of State
www.state.gov

Appendix B:
State Adoption Specialist, Photolisting, and Foster Care Information

State Adoption Specialist Offices

Each state has a governmental office that oversees the adoption process of that state. This office can provide information about complaints filed against private adoption agencies. It is also the office that oversees the placement of foster care children for adoption. This state office is the entity that will conduct the home study when you are going through the placement process for a public agency adoption.

This appendix contains each state's office for handling adoption along with its contact information. Nearly every state's office has a website, so you can gather even more information that is specific to your state on that site.

Alabama Department of Human Resources
Family Services Partnership, Office of Adoption
50 North Ripley Street
Montgomery, AL 36130–4000
334-242-1374
www.dhr.state.al.us

Alaska Department of Health and Social Services
Office of Children's Services
130 Seward Street, Room 406
P.O. Box 110630
Juneau, AK 99811-0630
907-465-3170
www.hss.state.ak.us/ocs/Adoptions

**Arizona Department of
Economic Security**
Children Need Homes
Division of Children, Youth, and
Families
P.O. Box 6123—Site Code 940A
Phoenix, AZ 85007
877-KIDSNEEDU
602-542-5499
www.de.state.az.us/dcyf/adoption/
default.asp

**Arkansas Department of Health and
Human Services**
P.O. Box 1437, Slot S565
Little Rock, AR 72203
888-736-2820
www.state.ar.us/dhs/adoption/
adoption.html

**California Department of
Social Services**
Child and Youth Permanency Branch
744 P Street—MS 19-69
Sacramento, CA 95814
916-651-7464
www.childsworld.ca.gov/
CFSDAdopti_309.htm

**Colorado Department of
Human Services (CDHS)**
1575 Sherman Street
Denver, CO 80203
303-866-5700
www.changealifeforever.org/
adoption.asp
www.cdhs.state.co.us

**Connecticut Department of
Children and Families**
Office of Foster and Adoption Services
505 Hudson Street
Hartford, CT 06106
860-550-6300
866-637-4737
www.ct.gov/dcf

**Delaware Department of Services for
Children, Youth and Their Families**
1825 Faulkland Road
Wilmington, DE 19805
302-633-2655
www.state.de.us/kids/information/
adoption.shtml

**District of Columbia Child and
Family Services Agency**
400 6th Street, SW
Washington, DC 20024
202-442-6000
www.cfsa.dc.gov

**Florida Department of
Children and Families**
1317 Winewood Boulevard
Building 1
Tallahassee, FL 32399
800-96-ADOPT
904-353-0679
www.dcf.state.fl.us/adoption

**Georgia Department of
Human Resources**
Division of Family and
Children Services
2 Peachtree Street, NW
Suite 18–486
Atlanta, GA 30303
404-657-3550
www.dfcs.dhr.georgia.gov

**Hawaii Department of
Human Services**
1390 Miller Street
Room 209
Honolulu, HI 96813
808-586-5698
www.hawaii.gov/dhs

**Idaho Department of
Health and Welfare**
Division of Family and
Community Services
450 West State Street, 5th Floor
Boise, ID 83720
800-926-2588
www.healthandwelfare.idaho.gov

**Illinois Department of Children and
Family Services**
Division of Foster Care and
Permanency Services
100 West Randolph—Suite 6–100
Chicago, IL 60601
312-814-6858
www.state.il.us/dcfs/adoption

**Indiana Division of
Family and Children**
Department of Child Services
Office of Communications
P.O. Box 7083
Indianapolis, IN 46207
888-25-ADOPT
www.in.gov/dcs/adoption

Iowa Department of Human Services
Hoover State Office Building
1305 East Walnut Avenue
Des Moines, IA 50319
515-281-5454
www.dhs.state.ia.us

**Kansas Department of Social and
Rehabilitation Services,**
Children and Family Policy Division
Docking State Office Building
915 SW Harrison
5th Floor South
Topeka, KS 66612
785-296-0918
www.srskansas.org/services/
adoption.htm

**Kentucky Cabinet for Health and
Family Services**
275 East Main Street
Frankfort, KY 40621
800-372-2973
http://cfc.state.ky.us/help/
adoption.asp

Louisiana Department of
  Social Services
Office of Community Services
627 North Fourth Street
Baton Rouge, LA 70801
225-342–2297
www.dss.state.la.us/departments/
  ocs/Adoption_Services.html

Maine Department of Health and
  Human Services
P.O. Box 754
Gardiner, ME 04345
877-505-0545
www.afamilyforme.org

Maryland Department of
  Human Resources
311 West Saratoga Street
Baltimore, MD 21201
800-39-ADOPT
www.dhr.state.md.us/ssa

Massachusetts Department of
  Social Services
24 Farnsworth Street
Boston, MA 02210
617-748–2000
www.mass.gov/dss

Michigan Department of
  Human Services
Child and Family Services
  Administration
P.O. Box 30037
Lansing, MI 48909
517-373–2035
www.michigan.gov/dhs

Minnesota Department of
  Human Services
Human Services Building
444 Lafayette Road
St. Paul, MN 55155
651-431–4656
www.dhs.state.mn.us

Mississippi Department of
  Human Services
Division of Family and Child Services
750 North State Street
Jackson, MS 39202
800-821-9157
www.mdhs.state.ms.us/
  fcs_adopt.html

Missouri Department of
  Social Services
Children's Division
615 Howerton Court
P.O. Box 88
Jefferson City, MO 65102
573-522–8024
www.dss.mo.gov/cd

Montana Department of Public
  Health and Human Services
Child and Family Services Division
1400 Broadway, Room C118
Helena, MT 59604
406-444–5900
www.dphhs.state.mt.gov

**Nebraska Department of
Health and Human Services**
P.O. Box 95044
Lincoln, NE 68509
402-471-2306
www.hhs.state.ne.us

**Nevada Department of
Human Resources**
Division of Child and Family Services
4126 Technology Way
3rd Floor
Carson City, NV 89706
775-684-4400
http://dcfs.state.nv.us

**New Hampshire Department of
Health and Human Services**
Division for Children,
Youth and Families
129 Pleasant Street—Brown Building
Concord, NH 03301
603-271-4711
www.dhhs.state.nh.us/dhhs/
fcadoption

**New Jersey Department of
Human Services—Division of
Youth and Family Services**
Office of Adoption Operations
P.O. Box 717
Trenton, NJ 08625
800-99-ADOPT
www.state.nj.us/njadopt

**New Mexico Children, Youth and
Families Department**
P.O. Drawer 5160
Santa Fe, NM 87502
800-432-2075
www.cyfd.org

New York State Adoption Service
Division of the Office of Children and
Family Services
52 Washington Street, Room 323 North
Rensselaer, NY 12144
800-345-5437
www.ocfs.state.ny.us/adopt

**North Carolina Department of
Health and Human Services**
Division of Social Services
2401 Mail Service Center
Raleigh, NC 27699
919-733-3055
www.dhhs.state.nc.us/dss/adoption

**North Dakota Department of
Human Services**
Children and Family Services Division
600 East Boulevard Avenue
Department 325
Bismarck, ND 58505
701-328-2316
www.nd.gov/humanservices/
services/childfamily/adoption

**Ohio Department of Job and
Family Services**
Office for Children and Families
255 East Main Street, 3rd Floor
Columbus, OH 43215
614-466–9274
http://jfs.ohio.gov/oapl

**Oklahoma Department of
Human Services**
Children and Family Services Division
907 South Detroit, Suite 750
Tulsa, OK 74120
918-588-1730
877-657-9438
www.okdhs.org/adopt

**Oregon Department of
Human Services — Office of
Permanency for Children and
of Training**
Human Services Building
Adoption Unit, 2nd Floor
500 Summer Street, NE
Salem, OR 97301
503-945–5944
www.oregon.gov/DHS

**Pennsylvania Department of
Public Welfare**
Office of Children, Youth and Families
P.O. Box 2675
Harrisburg, PA 17105
800-585–SWAN
www.dpw.state.pa.us/Child/
AdoptionFosterCare

**Rhode Island Department of
Children, Youth and Families**
Adoption & Foster Care
Preparation & Support
101 Friendship Street
Providence, RI 02903
401-528–3799
www.dcyf.ri.gov/adoption.php

**South Carolina Department of
Social Services**
Adoption & Birth Parent Services
1535 Confederate Avenue Extension
Columbia, SC 29202
800-922–2504
www.state.sc.us/dss/adoption

**South Dakota Department of
Social Services**
Department of Child
Protective Services
700 Governors Drive
Pierre, SD 57501
605-773–3165
www.dss.sd.gov

**Tennessee Department of
Children's Services**
Cordell Hull Building, 7th Floor
Nashville, TN 37243
877-DCS–KIDS
www.state.tn.us/youth/
adoption.htm

Texas Department of Family and Protective Services
P.O. Box 149030
Austin, TX 78714
800-233-3405
www.tdprs.state.tx.us/
Adoption_and_Foster_Care

Utah Department of Human Services
Division of Child and Family Services
120 North 200 West, Suite 225
Salt Lake City, UT 84103
801-538-4100
www.hsdcfs.utah.gov/adoption.htm

Vermont Family Services Division
Department for Children and Families
103 South Main Street
Waterbury, VT 05671
802-241-2131
www.path.state.vt.us/fsd

Virginia Department of Social Services
7 North 8th Street
Richmond, VA 23219
800-552-3431
www.dss.virginia.gov/family/ap

Washington Department of Social and Health Services
Division of Children and Family Services
P.O. Box 45130
Olympia, WA 98504
800-760-5340
www1.dshs.wa.gov/ca/adopt

West Virginia Department of Health and Human Resources
Office of Social Services
350 Capitol Street, Room 691
Charleston, WV 25301
304-558-2891
www.wvdhhr.org/oss/adoption/

Wisconsin Department of Health and Family Services
Division of Child and Family Services
1 West Wilson, Room 527
P.O. Box 8916
Madison, WI 53707
608-266-3595
www.dhfs.state.wi.us/children/
adoption

Wyoming Department of Family Services
130 Hobbs Avenue
Cheyenne, WY 82009
307-777-3570
http://dfsweb.state.wy.us/
adoption.html

State Adoption Photolisting Websites

The following sites contain photos and information about the children available for adoption in those states. Not every state offers this service.

ALASKA
Alaska Adoption Exchange
www.akae.org
www.hss.state.ak.us/ocs

ARKANSAS
Arkansas Adoption Resource Exchange
www.arkansas.gov/dhhs/adoption/
  adoption.html

ARIZONA
Arizona Department of
  Economic Security
www.de.state.az.us/dcyf/adoption/
  meet.asp

CALIFORNIA
California Kids Connection
www.cakidsconnection.com

COLORADO
The Adoption Exchange
www.adoptex.org

CONNECTICUT
Connecticut Department of
  Children and Families
www.adoptuskids.org/states/
  ct/index.aspx

DELAWARE
Adoption Center of Delaware Valley
www.acdv.org/waiting_children.html

DISTRICT OF COLUMBIA
District of Columbia Child and
  Family Services Agency
www.cfsa.dc.gov

GEORGIA
My Turn Now Photolisting
http://167.193.144.179/mtnmenu2.asp

IOWA
KidSake Foster/Adopt Iowa
www.iakids.org

ILLINOIS
Adoption Information
  Center of Illinois
www.adoptinfo-il.org

INDIANA
Indiana's Adoption Program
www.adoptachild.in.gov

KENTUCKY
Special Needs Adoption Program
  (SNAP)
https://apps.chfs.ky.gov/snap/

LOUISIANA
Louisiana Adoption
  Resource Exchange
www.adoptuskids.org/states/la

MASSACHUSETTS
Massachusetts Adoption
  Resource Exchange, Inc.
www.mareinc.org

MARYLAND
Maryland Adoption
  Resource Exchange
www.adoptuskids.org/states/md

MAINE
A Family for ME
www.afamilyforme.org/heart.html

MICHIGAN
Michigan Adoption
  Resource Exchange
www.mare.org

MINNESOTA
Minnesota Adoption
  Resource Network
www.mnadopt.org

MISSOURI
Missouri Adoption Photolisting
www.adoptuskids.org

MISSISSIPPI
Mississippi Adoption
  Resource Exchange
www.mdhs.state.ms.us/
  fcs_adopt.html

MONTANA
Montana Waiting
  Children Photolistings
www.adoptuskids.org/

NORTH CAROLINA
North Carolina Kids Adoption and
  Foster Care Network
www.adoptuskids.org/states/nc

NORTH DAKOTA
North Dakota Department of
  Human Services
www.state.nd.us/humanservices/
  services/childfamily/adoption/
  adoptuskids.html

NEW HAMPSHIRE
New Hampshire Department of
  Health and Human Services
www.dhhs.state.nh.us/dhhs/
  fcadoption

NEW JERSEY
New Jersey Division of Youth and
  Family Services Adoption Exchange
www.adoptuskids.org/states/nj

NEW MEXICO
New Mexico Children, Youth, and
  Families Department
www.cyfd.org

NEVADA
Nevada Photolisting Service
http://dcfs.state.nv.us

NEW YORK
New York State Office of
  Children and Family Services
www.ocfs.state.ny.us/adopt

OHIO
AdoptOHIO
www.jfs.ohio.gov/oapl

OREGON
Oregon's Waiting Children
www.nwae.org/wait-or.html

PENNSYLVANIA
Pennsylvania Adoption Exchange
www.adoptpakids.org

RHODE ISLAND
Adoption Rhode Island
www.adoptionri.org

SOUTH CAROLINA
South Carolina Council on
  Adoptable Children
www.sc-adopt.org

TENNESSEE
Tennesse Department of
  Children's Services
www.state.tn.us/youth/adoption.htm

TEXAS
Texas Adoption Resource Exchange
www.adoptchildren.org

UTAH
Utah Adoption Connection
www.utdcfsadopt.org

VIRGINIA
Virginia Department of
  Social Services
www.adoptuskids.org/states/va

VERMONT
Project Family
www.projectfamilyvt.org/
  adoption.html

WASHINGTON
Washington Adoption
  Resource Exchange
www.warekids.org

WEST VIRGINIA
West Virginia Adoption
  Resource Network
www.adoptawvchild.org

WYOMING
Wyoming Department of
  Family Services
http://dfsweb.state.wy.us/
  adoption.html

State Foster Care Website Pages

The following websites contain information about foster care programs in each state.

ALASKA
Alaska Office of Children's Services
www.hss.state.ak.us/ocs/FosterCare/
default.htm

ALABAMA
Alabama Department of
  Human Resources
www.dhr.state.al.us

ARKANSAS
Arkansas Department of
  Human Services
www.arkansas.gov/dhhs/chilnfam/
FosterFamilies.htm

ARIZONA
Arizona Department of
  Economic Security
www.de.state.az.us/dcyf/adoption/
information.asp

CALIFORNIA
California Department of
  Social Services
www.childsworld.ca.gov/
FosterCare_310.htm

COLORADO
Colorado State Department of
  Human Services
www.changealifeforever.org/foster.asp

CONNECTICUT
Connecticut Department of
  Children and Families
www.ct.gov/dcf

DELAWARE
Delaware Department of
  Services for Children, Youth and
  Their Families
www.state.de.us/kids/fs/
fostercare.shtml

DISTRICT OF COLUMBIA
District of Columbia
  Department of Human Services
http://dhs.dc.gov/dhs

FLORIDA
Florida Department of
  Children and Families
www.dcf.state.fl.us/fostercare/

GEORGIA
Georgia Department of
  Human Resources
www.dfcs.dhr.georgia.gov

HAWAII
Hawaii Department of
  Human Services
www.hawaii.gov/dhs

IOWA
Iowa Kidsake Foster/Adopt Iowa
www.iakids.org/foster_care/
fostercare.asp

IDAHO
Idaho Department of
Health and Welfare
www.healthandwelfare.idaho.gov

ILLINOIS
Illinois Department of
Children and Family Services
www.state.il.us/dcfs/foster

INDIANA
Indiana Department of Child Services
www.in.gov/dcs/foster

KANSAS
Kansas Department of
Social and Rehabilitation Services
www.srskansas.org/services/
fostercare.htm

KENTUCKY
Kentucky Cabinet for
Health and Family Services
http://chfs.ky.gov/dcbs/dpp/
Foster+Care+and+Adoption+
Programs.htm

LOUISIANA
Louisiana Department of
Social Services
www.dss.state.la.us/departments/
ocs/Foster_Parents.html

MASSACHUSETTS
Massachusetts Department of
Social Services
www.mass.gov/dss

MARYLAND
Maryland Department of
Human Resources
www.dhr.state.md.us/ssa/
foster/index.htm

MAINE
Maine Department of
Health and Human Services
www.maine.gov/dhhs/bcfs/
fosteradopt.htm

MICHIGAN
Michigan Department of
Human Services
www.michigan.gov/dhs

MINNESOTA
Minnesota Department of
Human Services
www.dhs.state.mn.us

MISSOURI
Missouri Department of
Social Services
www.dss.mo.gov/cd/fostercare/

MISSISSIPPI
Mississippi Department of
Human Services
www.mdhs.state.ms.us/fcs_foster.html

MONTANA
Montana Department of
  Public Health and Human Services
www.dphhs.mt.gov

NORTH CAROLINA
North Carolina Department of
  Social Services
www.dhhs.state.nc.us/dss/fostercare

NORTH DAKOTA
North Dakota Department of
  Human Services
www.state.nd.us/humanservices/
  services/childfamily/fostercare/

NEBRASKA
Nebraska Health and
  Human Services System
www.hhs.state.ne.us/chs/foc/
  focindex.htm

NEW HAMPSHIRE
New Hampshire Department of
  Health and Human Services
www.dhhs.state.nh.us/dhhs/
  fcadoption/default.htm

NEW JERSEY
New Jersey Department of
  Human Services
www.state.nj.us/njfostercare

NEW MEXICO
New Mexico Department of
  Children, Youth, and Families
www.cyfd.org

NEVADA
Nevada Division of Child &
  Family Services
www.dcfs.state.nv.us/DCFS_
  PlaceRes.htm

NEW YORK
New York State Office of
  Children and Family Services
www.ocfs.state.ny.us/main/fostercare

OHIO
Ohio Department of Job and
  Family Services
http://jfs.ohio.gov/factsheets/
  fostercare.pdf

OKLAHOMA
Oklahoma Department of
  Human Services
www.okdhs.org/fostercare

OREGON
Oregon Department of
  Human Services
www.oregon.gov/DHS/children/
  fostercare

PENNSYLVANIA
Pennsylvania Department of
  Public Welfare
www.dpw.state.pa.us/child/
  adoptionfostercare

RHODE ISLAND
Rhode Island Department of
  Children, Youth, and Families
www.dcyf.ri.gov/foster

SOUTH CAROLINA
South Carolina Department of
  Social Services
www.state.sc.us/dss/fostercare

SOUTH DAKOTA
South Dakota Department of
  Social Services
www.dss.sd.gov/fostercare

TENNESSEE
Tennessee Department of
  Children's Services
www.state.tn.us/youth/fostercare

TEXAS
Texas Adoption Resource Exchange
www.tdprs.state.tx.us/Adoption_
  and_Foster_Care/About_Foster_
  Care/default.asp

UTAH
Utah Department of Human Services
www.hsdcfs.utah.gov/foster_care.htm

VIRGINIA
Virginia Department of
  Social Services
www.dss.virginia.gov/family/fc

VERMONT
Vermont Project Family
http://projectfamilyvt.org/
  fosterCare.html

WASHINGTON
Washington Department of
  Social and Health Services
www1.dshs.wa.gov/ca/
  fosterparents

WISCONSIN
Wisconsin Department of
  Health and Family Services
http://dhfs.wisconsin.gov/
  children/foster

WEST VIRGINIA
West Virginia Department of
  Health and Human Resources
www.wvdhhr.org/bcf/children_
  adult/foster/

WYOMING
Wyoming Department of Family
Services
http://dfsweb.state.wy.us/FosterCare.
html

Appendix C:
Sample Adoption Forms

This appendix contains sample forms for various types of adoption. These forms are for example purposes only. You should always contact an attorney and be sure to use the current, up-to-date forms required in your state.

D.R.L. §§ 111-a(1), 112

Form 1-A
(Adoption
Petition-Agency)
(9/2006)

FAMILY COURT OF THE STATE OF NEW YORK
COUNTY OF
....
In the Matter of the Adoption of
A Child Whose First Name is

(Docket)(File) No.

PETITION FOR
ADOPTION
(Agency)

....

The Petitioner(s) respectfully allege(s) to this Court that [Delete inapplicable provisions]:

    1. Petitioning adoptive parent [specify name]:

        a. resides at [specify address, including county]:

        b. is of full age, having been born on [specify date of birth]:

        c. is   ☐ unmarried

              ☐ married to [specify name]:   and living together;

              ☐ married to [specify name]:   and living separate and apart
pursuant to a decree or judgment of separation or pursuant to a separation agreement subscribed by the
parties thereto and acknowledged or proved in the form required to entitle a deed to be recorded;

              ☐ married to [specify name]:   and living separate and
apart for at least three years prior to commencement of the proceeding);

        d. is of the following religious faith, if any [specify]:

        e. is engaged in the following occupation [specify]:   and earns
$ in approximate annual income [delete if inapplicable]: of which $ is
support and maintenance to be received from the Commissioner of Social Services on behalf of the
adoptive child.

    2. Petitioning adoptive parent [specify name]:

        a. resides at [specify address, including county]:

        b. is of full age, having been born on [specify date of birth]:

        c. is   ☐ unmarried

              ☐ married to [specify name]:   and living together;

              ☐ married to [specify name]:   and living separate and apart
pursuant to a decree or judgment of separation or pursuant to a separation agreement subscribed by the
parties thereto and acknowledged or proved in the form required to entitle a deed to be recorded;

206

Adoption Form 1-A   Page 2

□ married to [specify name]:   and living separate and
apart for at least three years prior to commencement of the proceeding);

        d. is of the following religious faith [specify]:

        e. is engaged in the following occupation [specify]:
and earns $ in approximate annual income [delete if inapplicable]: of which $
        is support and maintenance to be received from the Commissioner of Social Services on
behalf of the adoptive child.

    3. Upon information and belief, the adoptive child, whose first name is [specify]:

was born on   ,   , at   and the religious faith of such child is [specify]:

.

    4. Upon information and belief, there will be annexed to this petition a schedule verified by a
duly constituted official of [specify agency]:   , an authorized agency, as required
by section 112(3)of the Domestic Relations Law, concerning the adoptive child who is the subject of
this proceeding.

    5. The following is information, as nearly as can be ascertained, concerning the birth or legal
parents of the adoptive child:

       (a)   Age and date of birth

Parent [specify name]:
Parent [specify name]:

       (b)   Heritage (specify nationality, ethnic background, race)

Parent [specify name]:
Parent [specify name]:

       (c)   Religious faith, if any

Parent [specify name]:
Parent [specify name]:

       (d)   Education [specify number of years of school or degrees completed at time of
birth of adoptive child]:

Parent [specify name]:
Parent [specify name]:

       (e)   General physical appearance at time of birth of adoptive child [specify height,
weight, color of hair, eyes, skin]:
Parent [type name]:
        Ht:_____ Wt:_____
        Hair Color:_____ Eye Color: _____
        Skin Color: _____

Parent [type name]:
        Ht:_____ Wt:_____
        Hair Color:_____ Eye Color: _____
        Skin Color: _____

(f) Annex Form 1-D which provides health and medical history of birth parents at time of birth of adoptive child, including conditions or diseases believed to be hereditary and any drugs or medication taken during pregnancy by child's mother.

(g) Specify any other information which may be a factor influencing the adoptive child's present or future well-being, including talents, hobbies and special interests of parents: [attach separate sheet if necessary]

6. The subject child ❑ is ❑ is not a Native-American child, who is subject to the Indian Child Welfare Act of 1978 (25 U.S.C. §§ 1901-1963). If so, the following have been notified [check applicable box(es)]:
❑ parent/custodian [specify name and give notification date]:
❑ tribe/nation [specify name and give notification date]:
❑ United States Secretary of the Interior [give notification date]:

7. The manner in which the adoptive parent(s) obtained the adoptive child is as follows:

[Delete if inapplicable]: 8. The placement is subject to the provisions of section(s) ❑374-a ❑ 382 of the Social Services Law and the provisions of such sections have been complied with. The original approval signed by the Administrator of the Interstate Compact on the placement of Children is attached hereto.

9. The adoptive child resided with the adoptive parent(s) from [specify date]:

10. Other persons living in the household are [specify names and dates of birth]:

11.   The name by which the adoptive child is to be known is:

12.   Upon information and belief, the adoptive child ❑has   ❑has not   been previously adopted.

13. To the best of Petitioner(s)' information and belief, there are no persons other than those mentioned herein or in the verified schedule annexed hereto who are entitled, pursuant to Sections 111(3) and 111-a of the Domestic Relations Law, to notice of this proceeding (except):

Name: Relationship:
Last known address:

Name: Relationship:
Last known address:

Name   Relationship:
Last known address:

14 (a). The adoptive parent(s) ❑(has)(have) ❑ (has)(have) no   knowledge that the child or an adoptive parent is the subject of an indicated report, or is another person named in an indicated report of child abuse or maltreatment, as such terms are defined in section 412 of the Social Services Law, or has been the subject of or the respondent in a child protective proceeding which resulted in an order

finding that the child is an abused or neglected child.

(b)[Check applicable box(es)]: Upon information and belief,
☐ Neither the adoptive parent(s) nor any other adult over the age of 18 residing in the household have a criminal record.
☐ The following adoptive parent(s)[specify]:   have been convicted of the following offenses [specify, including dates) of conviction]:
However, denial of Petitioner's petition will create an unreasonable risk of harm to the physical or mental health of the child and granting the petition will not place the child's safety in jeopardy and will be in the best interests of the child, pursuant to Social Services Law §378-a(2)(e)(1), for the following reason(s) [specify]:

☐ The following adult over the age of 18 living in the home [specify]:
has the following record of criminal conviction(s) [specify, including date(s)]:

15.   There are no prior or pending proceedings affecting the custody or status of the adoptive child, including any proceeding[s] dismissed or withdrawn, (except)[specify type of proceeding, court, disposition, if any, and date of disposition, if any]:

[If there is a post-adoption contact agreement, attach it and answer Question 16]:
16 ☐ On [specify date]:   , at the time of the approval of the surrender of the child, the Family Court, [specify]:   County, approved the annexed post-adoption contact agreement as being in the child's best interests. The agreement was consented to in writing by the following [specify]:
Adoptive parent(s)[specify]:
Birth parent(s) [specify]:
Adoptive child's law guardian [specify]:
Sibling(s) or half-sibling(s) over the age of 14, if contact is with siblings or half-siblings [specify]:

17. This petition ☐ has ☐ has not been filed in the Court that exercised jurisdiction over the most recent permanency or other proceeding involving this child. [If it has not, petitioner must file affirmation, Adoption Form 1-E].

18. [Insert any additional allegations.]

WHEREFORE, the Petitioner(s) requests an order:
approving the adoption of the adoptive child [specify first name]:   by the Petitioner(s), and [delete if inapplicable]: incorporating the post-adoption contact agreement,   and
directing that the adoptive child shall be treated in all respects as the child of the Petitioner(s), and directing that the name of the adoptive child be changed and that (s)he shall henceforth be known by the name of [specify]:   , together with such other and further relief as may be just and proper.

Dated: ,   .

_____/_____
Adoptive Parent: typed or printed name/ signature

_____/_____
Adoptive Parent: typed or printed name / signature

_____/_____
Adoptive child if over 18: typed or printed name/ signature[1]

_____/_____
Attorney if any: typed or printed name/signature

_____
Attorney's Address and Telephone number

---

[1] If the child is over the age of 14, written consent to the adoption must also be attached.

VERIFICATION

STATE OF NEW YORK   )
                                          :ss.:

COUNTY OF   )

being duly sworn, says that (he)(she) (they)(is)(are) the Petitioner(s) in the above-named proceeding
and that the foregoing petition is true to (his)(her)(their) own knowledge, except as to matters where in
stated to be alleged on information and belief and as to those matters (he)(she) (they) believe(s) it to be
true.

_____/_____
Adoptive Parent: typed or printed name/ signature

_____/_____
Adoptive Parent: typed or printed name/ signature

_____/_____
Adoptive child if over 18: typed or printed name/ signature

Sworn to before me this
      day of   ,   .

_____
(Deputy)Clerk of the Court
      Notary Public

Resworn to before me this
      day of   ,   .

_____
Judge of the   Court

THE STATE OF NEW HAMPSHIRE
JUDICIAL BRANCH
http://www.courts.state.nh.us

Court Name: _____

Case Name: Surrender of Parental Rights over _____

Case Number: _____
(if known)

SURRENDER OF PARENTAL RIGHTS

Of: ☐ Birth Mother ☐ Birth Father ☐ Legal Father
(RSA 170-B:5 through 170-B:12)

1. Name of parent surrendering rights _____

   Telephone _____ City/town, state of residence _____

   Mailing Address _____

   Date of Birth _____ Place of Birth _____

2. Attorney for surrendering parent _____ Telephone _____

   Mailing Address _____

3. Name of other parent _____

   Telephone _____ City/town, state of residence _____

   Mailing Address _____

   Date of Birth _____ Place of Birth _____

4. Child Name _____

   Date of Birth _____ Place of Birth _____

5. Is the child an Indian child as defined by the Indian Child Welfare Act? ☐ Yes ☐ No
   If yes, name and address of tribe _____

   Is tribe recognized by the federal government as eligible for federal services or certain Alaskan native corporations as defined in 43 U.S.C. §1602(c)? ☐ Yes ☐ No

6. Birth mother's marital status: ☐ Single ☐ Married ☐ Divorced ☐ Widowed
   If married, divorced or widowed, name of spouse _____
   If applicable, date of marriage _____ date of divorce _____

7. Do you know the identity of the adoptive parents? ☐ Yes ☐ No

8. Are there any pending adoption, juvenile, domestic violence, marriage dissolution, domestic relations, paternity, legitimation, custody or other proceedings affecting minor or parents of this minor? ☐ Yes ☐ No If yes, attach a separate sheet identifying and explaining each.

Case Name: Surrender of Parental Rights over _____
Case Number: _____
SURRENDER OF PARENTAL RIGHTS _____

Please read carefully or complete the information below before signing this document.

By completing this surrender of parental rights, I understand that my parental rights over the child, including the rights of care, custody and control of the child, will cease when the court approves this surrender. I also waive any right to receive any notices about future hearings about the child.

I understand that after the court approves this surrender, all my parental obligations will be extinguished, except the obligation to pay any accrued unpaid child support.

I understand that after the court approves this surrender in compliance with New Hampshire law, the surrender is final, and may not be revoked or set aside for any reason, unless the court finds that the surrender was obtained by fraud or duress, and that the withdrawal of the surrender is in the best interests of the adoptee. The failure of an adoptive parent to comply with an arrangement or understanding reached with the birth parent with respect to the post-surrender exchange of identifying or non-identifying information, communication or contact is not a reason to revoke or set aside a surrender.

I have been informed that child placing agencies duly licensed pursuant to RSA 170-E are available to counsel me about my decision to surrender my parental rights.

I have been provided legal counsel, unless waived with approval of the court.

I have not received or been promised any money or anything of value for the completion of this surrender, except for payments permissible under New Hampshire law. They are as follows:

_____

_____

By signing this document below, I declare:

- that I am the parent of the above named child;
- that all the information on this surrender form is true;
- that I have read and understand the content of this document;
- that all of my questions have been answered by the court or its designee;
- that I wish this surrender of parental rights to take effect; and
- that (please check one of the following):
  ☐ I do not wish to receive confirmation of the final adoption of this child.
  ☐ I wish to receive confirmation of the final adoption of this child.

_____   _____
Date   Signature

State of _____, County of _____

This instrument was acknowledged before me on _____ by _____

My Commission Expires _____
Affix Seal, if any   Signature of Judge / Notarial Officer / Title

212

Case Name: Surrender of Parental Rights over _____
Case Number: _____
<u>SURRENDER OF PARENTAL RIGHTS</u> _____

| If the surrendering parent is a minor or under guardianship, complete the following section. |

We, _____, are the parents or guardians of the
named birth parent who is surrendering his/her rights, and hereby give our assent to this surrender.

_____   _____
Signature / Relationship   Address

_____   _____
Signature / Relationship   Address

State of _____, County of _____

This instrument was acknowledged before me on _____ by _____

My Commission Expires _____   _____
Affix Seal, if any   Signature of Notarial Officer / Title

| ORDER |

This surrender of parental rights is: ☐ Approved   ☐ Not approved

_____   _____
Date   Judge

OMB No. 1615-0028; Expires 08/31/08

I-600, Petition to Classify Orphan as an Immediate Relative

Department of Homeland Security
U.S. Citizenship and Immigration Services

Do not write in this block.	**(For USCIS Use Only.)**

TO THE SECRETARY OF STATE:

The petition was filed by:

☐ Married petitioner   ☐ Unmarried petitioner

The petition is approved for orphan:

☐ Adopted abroad   ☐ Coming to U.S. for adoption. Preadoption requirements have been met.

Fee Stamp

Remarks:

File number

DATE OF ACTION

DD

DISTRICT

Type or print legibly in black ink. Complete a separate petition for each child.
Petition is being made to classify the named orphan as an immediate relative

Block I - Information about petitioner.

1. My name is: (Last)   (First)   (Middle)

2. Other names used (including maiden name if appropriate):

3. I reside in the U.S. at: (C/O if appropriate)   (Apt. No.)

   (Number and Street)   (Town or City)   (State) (Zip Code)

4. Address Abroad (if any):   (Number and Street)   (Apt. No.)

   (Town or city)   (Province)   (Country)

5. I was born on: (mm/dd/yyyy)

   In: (Town or City)   (State or Province)   (Country)

6. My telephone number is: (Include Area Code)

7. My marital status is:

   ☐ Married
   ☐ Widowed
   ☐ Divorced
   ☐ Single
       ☐ I have never been married.
       ☐ I have been previously married _____ time(s).

8. If you are now married, give the following information:

   Date and place of present marriage (mm/dd/yyyy)

   Name of present spouse (include maiden name of wife)

   Date of birth of spouse (mm/dd/yyyy) Place of birth of spouse

   Number of prior marriages of spouse

   My spouse resides   ☐ With me   ☐ Apart from me (provide address below)

   (Apt. No.) (No. and Street)   (City)   (State) (Country)

9. I am a citizen of the United States through:

   ☐ Birth   ☐ Parents   ☐ Naturalization

   If acquired through naturalization, give name under which naturalized, number of naturalization certificate, and date and place of naturalization:

   If not, submit evidence of citizenship. See Instruction 2.a(2).

   If acquired through parentage, have you obtained a certificate in your own name based on that acquisition?
   ☐ No   ☐ Yes

   Have you or any person through whom you claimed citizenship ever lost U.S. citizenship?
   ☐ No   ☐ Yes (If Yes, attach detailed explanation.)

Received	Trans. In	Ret'd Trans. Out	Completed

214

Block II - Information about orphan beneficiary.

10. Name at Birth (First) (Middle) (Last)

11. Name at Present (First) (Middle) (Last)

12. Any other names by which orphan is or was known.

13. Gender ☐ Male **14.** Date of birth (mm/dd/yyyy)
☐ Female

15. Place of Birth (City) (State or Province) (Country)

16. The beneficiary is an orphan because (check one):
☐ He or she has no parents.
☐ He or she has only one parent who is the sole or surviving parent.

17. If the orphan has only one parent, answer the following:
a. State what has become of the other parent:

b. Is the remaining parent capable of providing for the orphan's
support? ☐ Yes ☐ No
c. Has the remaining parent in writing irrevocably released the
orphan for emigration and adoption? ☐ Yes ☐ No

18. Has the orphan been adopted abroad by the petitioner and spouse
jointly or the unmarried petitioner? ☐ Yes ☐ No
If yes, did the petitioner and spouse or unmarried petitioner
personally see and observe the child prior to or during the
adoption proceedings? ☐ Yes ☐ No
Date of adoption (mm/dd/yyyy)

Place of adoption

19. If either answer in Question 18 is "No," answer the following:
a. Do petitioner and spouse jointly or does the unmarried petitioner
intend to adopt the orphan in the United States?
☐ Yes ☐ No
b. Have the preadoption requirements, if any, of the orphan's
proposed State of residence been met? ☐ Yes ☐ No
c. If **b** is answered "No," will they be met later?
☐ Yes ☐ No

20. To petitioner's knowledge, does the orphan have any physical or mental
affliction? ☐ Yes ☐ No
If "Yes," name the affliction.

21. Who has legal custody of the child?

22. Name of child welfare agency, if any, assisting in this case:

23. Name of attorney abroad, if any, representing petitioner in this case.
Address of above.

24. Address in the United States where orphan will reside.

25. Present address of orphan.

25. If orphan is residing in an institution, give full name of institution.

26. If orphan is not residing in an institution, give full name of person with
with whom residing.

27. Give any additional information necessary to locate orphan, such as
name of district, section, zone or locality in which orphan resides.

28. Location of American embassy or consulate where application for visa
will be made.

(City in Foreign Country) (Foreign Country)

Certification of petitioner.
I certify, under penalty of perjury under the laws of the United States of
America, that the foregoing is true and correct and that I will care for an
orphan or orphans properly if admitted to the United States.

(Signature of Petitioner)

Executed on (Date)

Certification of married prospective petitioner's spouse.
I certify, under penalty of perjury under the laws of the United States of
America, that the foregoing is true and correct and that my spouse and I
will care for an orphan or orphans properly if admitted to the United States.

(Signature of Petitioner)

Executed on (Date)

Signature of person preparing form, if other than petitioner.
I declare that this document was prepared by me at the request of the petitioner and is
based entirely on information of which I have knowledge.

(Signature)

Street Address and Room or Suite No./City/State/Zip Code

Executed on (Date)

Form I-600 (Rev. 10/26/05)Y Page 2

OMB No. 1615-0028; Expires 08/31/08

Department of Homeland Security
U.S. Citizenship and Immigration Services

I-600, Petition to Classify Orphan
as an Immediate Relative

Instructions

1. Eligibility.

A. Child.

Under immigration law, an orphan is an alien child who has no parents because of the death or disappearance of abandonment or desertion by, or separation or loss from both parents.

An orphan is also an alien child who has only one parent who is not capable of taking care of the orphan and who has in writing irrevocably released the alien for emigration and adoption.

A petition to classify an alien as an orphan may not be filed on behalf of a child in the United States, unless that child is in parole status and has not been adopted in the United States.

The petition must be filed before the child's 16th birthday.

B. Parent(s).

The petition may be filed by a married U.S. citizen and spouse or unmarried U.S. citizen at least 25 years of age. The spouse does not need to be a U.S. citizen, but must be in lawful immigration status.

C. Adoption abroad.

If the orphan was adopted abroad, it must be established that both the married petitioner and spouse or the unmarried petitioner personally saw and observed the child prior to or during the adoption proceedings. The adoption decree must show that a married petitioner and spouse adopted the child jointly or that an unmarried petitioner was at least 25 years of age at the time of the adoption.

D. Proxy adoption abroad.

If both the petitioner and spouse or the unmarried petitioner did not personally see and observe the child prior to or during the adoption proceedings abroad, the petitioner (and spouse, if married) must submit a statement indicating the petitioner's (and, if married, the spouse's) willingness and intent to readopt the child in the United States.

If requested by USCIS, the petitioner must submit a statement by an official of the State in which the child will reside that readoption is permissible in that State In addition, evidence of compliance with the preadoption requirements, if any, of that State must be submitted.

E. Preadoption requirements.

If the orphan has not been adopted abroad, the petitioner and spouse or the unmarried petitioner must establish that:

- The child will be adopted in the United States by the petitioner and spouse jointly or by the unmarried petitioner, and that
- The preadoption requirements, if any, of the State of the orphan's proposed residence have been met.

2. Filing Petition for Known Child.

An orphan petition for a child who has been identified must be submitted on a completed Form I-600 with the certification of the petitioner executed and required fee. If the petitioner is married, the Form I-600 must also be signed by the petitioner's spouse.

The petition must be accompanied by the following:

A. Proof of U.S. citizenship of the petitioner.

If a U.S. citizen by birth in the United States, submit a copy of the birth certificate, issued by the civil registrar, vital statistics office or other civil authority. If a birth certificate is not available, submit a statement from the appropriate civil authority certifying that a birth certificate is not available. In such a situation, secondary evidence must be submitted, including:

- **Church records** bearing the seal of the church showing the baptism, dedication or comparable rite occurred within two months after birth and showing the date and place of the petitioner's birth, date of the religious ceremony and the names of the parents;

- **School records** issued by the authority (preferably the first school attended) showing the date of admission to the school, the petitioner's birth date or age at the time, the place of birth and the names of the parents;

- **Census records** (state or federal) showing the name, place of birth, date of birth or age of the petitioner listed;

- **Affidavits** sworn to or affirmed by two persons who were living at the time and who have personal knowledge of the date and place of birth in the United States of the petitioner. Each affidavit should contain the following information regarding the person making the affidavit: his or her full name, address, date and place of birth and relationship to the petitioner, if any, and full information concerning the event and complete details of how the affiant acquired knowledge of petitioner's birth; or

- An unexpired **U.S. passport**, initially issued for ten years may also be submitted as proof of U.S. citizenship.

If the petitioner was born outside the United States, submit a copy of one of the following:

- Certificate of Naturalization or Certificate of Citizenship issued by the U.S. Citizenship and Immigration Services (USCIS) or former Immigration and Naturalization Service (INS);

- Form FS-240, Report of Birth Abroad of a Citizen of the United States, issued by an American embassy;

- An unexpired U.S. passport initially issued for ten years, or

- An original statement from a U.S. consular officer verifying the applicant's U.S. citizenship with a valid passport.

NOTE: Proof of the lawful immigration status of the petitioner's spouse, if applicable, must be submitted. If the spouse is not a U.S. citizen, proof of the spouse's lawful immigration status, such as Form I-551, Permanent Resident Card; Form I-94, Arrival-Departure Record; or a copy of the biographic pages of the spouse's passport and the nonimmigrant visa pages showing an admission stamp may be submitted.

B. Proof of marriage of petitioner and spouse.

The married petitioner must submit a copy of the certificate of marriage and proof of termination of all prior marriages of himself or herself and spouse. In the case of an unmarried petitioner who was previously married, submit proof of termination of all prior marriages.

NOTE: If any change occurs in the petitioner's marital status while the case is pending, immediately notify the USCIS office where the petition was filed.

C. Proof of age of orphan.

The petitioner should submit a copy of the orphan's birth certificate if obtainable; if not obtainable, submit an explanation together with the best available evidence of birth.

D. Copies of the death certificate(s) of the child's parent(s) if applicable.

E. A certified copy of adoption decree together with certified translation, if the orphan has been lawfully adopted abroad.

F. Evidence that the sole or surviving parent is incapable of providing for the orphan's care and has in writing irrevocably released the orphan for immigration and adoption, if the orphan has only one parent.

G. Evidence that the orphan has been unconditionally abandoned to an orphanage, if the orphan has been placed in an orphanage by his or her parent or parents.

H. Evidence that the preadoption requirements, if any, of the state of the orphan's proposed residence have been met, if the child is to be adopted in the United States.

If is not possible to submit this evidence upon initial filing of the petition under the laws of the State of proposed residence, it may be submitted later. The petition, however, will not be approved without it.

I. Home Study.

The home study must include a statement or attachment recommending or approving the adoption or proposed adoption and be signed by an official of the responsible State agency in the State of the proposed residence or of an agency authorized by that State. In the case of a child adopted abroad, the statement or attachment must be signed by an official of an appropriate public or private adoption agency that is licensed in the United States.

The home study must be prepared by an entity (individual or organization) licensed or otherwise authorized under the law of the State of the orphan's proposed residence to conduct research and preparation for a home study, including the required personal interviews.

If the recommending entity is licensed, the recommendation must state that it is licensed, where it is licensed, its license number, if any, and the period of validity of the license.

However, the research, including the interview and the preparation of the home study, may be done by an individual or group in the United States or abroad that is satisfactory to the recommending entity.

A responsible State agency or licensed agency may accept a home study made by an unlicensed or foreign agency and use that home study as a basis for a favorable recommendation.

The home study must provide an assessment of the capabilities of the prospective adoptive parent(s) to properly parent the orphan and must include a discussion of the following areas:

- An explanation regarding any history of abuse or violence or any complaints, charges, citations, arrests, convictions, prison terms, pardons rehabilitation decrees for breaking or violating any law or ordinance by the petitioner(s) or any additional adult member of the household over age 18.

NOTE: Having committed any crime of moral turpitude or a drug-related offense does not necessarily mean that a petitioner or petitioner's spouse will be found ineligible to adopt an orphan. However, failure to disclose such information may result in denial of this application and/or any subsequent petition for an orphan.

- An assessment of the financial ability of the petitioner and petitioner's spouse, if applicable.

- A detailed description of the living accommodations where the petitioner and petitioner's spouse currently reside(s).

- If the petitioner and petitioner's spouse are residing abroad at the time of the home study, a description of the living accommodations where the child will reside in the United States with the petitioner and petitioner's spouse, if known.

- An assessment of the physical, mental and emotional capabilities of the petitioner and petitioner's spouse in relation to rearing and educating the child.

J. Biometric services.

As part of the USCIS biometric services requirements, the following persons must be fingerprinted in connection with this petition:

- The petitioner and petitioner's spouse, if applicable, and

- Each additional adult member the petitioner's household, 18 years of age or older. **NOTE:** Submit a copy of the birth certificate of each household member over 18.

If necessary, USCIS may also take a photograph and signature of those named above as part of the biometric services.

Petitioners residing in the United States. After filing this petition, USCIS will notify each person in writing of the time and location where they must go to be fingerprinted. Failure to appear to be fingerprinted or for other biometric services may result in denial of the petition.

Petitioners residing abroad. Completed fingerprint cards (Forms FD-258) must be submitted with the petition. Do not, bend, fold or crease completed fingerprint cards. Fingerprint cards must be prepared by a U.S. embassy or consulate, USCIS office or military installation.

3. Filing Petition for Known Child Without Full Documentation on Child or Home Study.

When a child has been identified but the documentary evidence relating to the child or the home study is not yet available, an orphan petition may be filed without that evidence or home study.

The evidence outlined in Instructions **2A** and **2B** (proof of petitioner's U.S. citizenship and documentation of marriage of petitioner and spouse), however, must be submitted.

If the necessary evidence relating to the child or the home study is not submitted within one year from the date of submission of the petition, the petition will be considered abandoned and the fee will not be refunded. Any further proceeding will require the filing of a new petition.

4. Submitting Advance Processing Application for Orphan Child Not Yet Identified.

A prospective petitioner may request advance processing when the child has not been identified or when the prospective petitioner and/or spouse is or are going abroad to locate or adopt a child.

If unmarried, the prospective petitioner must be at least 24 years of age, provided that he or she will be at least 25 at the time of the adoption and the completed petition on behalf of a child is filed.

The request must be on Form I-600A, Application for Advance Processing of Orphan Petition, and accompanied by the evidence requested on that form.

After a child or children are located and/or identified, a separate Form I-600 must be filed for each child. If only one Form I-600 is filed, a new fee is not required, provided the form is filed while the advance processing application (Form I-600A) application is pending or within 18 months of the approval of the advance processing application.

5. When Child/Children Are Located and/or Identified.

A separate Form I-600, Petition to Classify Orphan as an Immediate Relative, must be filed for each child.

Generally, Form I-600 should be submitted at the USCIS office where the advance processing application was filed.

If a prospective petitioner goes abroad to adopt or locate a child in one of the countries noted below, he or she should file Form I-600 at the USCIS office having jurisdiction over the place where the child is residing or will be located, unless the case is retained at the stateside office.

USCIS has offices in the following countries: Austria, China, Cuba, the Dominican Republic, El Salvador, Germany, Ghana, Great Britain, Greece, Guatemala, Haiti Honduras, India, Italy, Jamaica, Kenya, Korea, Mexico, Pakistan, Panama, Peru, the Philippines, Russia, South Africa, Thailand and Vietnam.

If a prospective petitioner goes abroad to any country not listed above to adopt or locate a child he or she should file Form I-600 at the American embassy or consulate having jurisdiction over the place where the child is residing or will be located, unless the case is retained at the Stateside office.

6. General Filing Instructions.

A. Type or print legibly in black ink.

B. If extra space is needed to complete any item, attach a continuation sheet, indicate the item number, and date and sign each sheet.

C. Translations.

Any foreign language document must be accompanied by a full English translation, that the translator has certified as complete and correct, and by the translator's certification that he or she is competent to translate the foreign language.

D. Copies.

If these instructions tell you to submit a copy of a particular document, you do not have to send the original document. However, if there are stamps, remarks, notations, etc., on the back of the original documents, also submit copies of the back of the document(s). You do not have to submit the original document unless USCIS requests it.

There are times when USCIS must request an original copy of a document. In that case, the original is generally returned after it has been reviewed.

7. Filing the Petition.

A petitioner residing in the United States should send the completed petition to the USCIS office having jurisdiction over his or her place of residence. A petitioner residing outside the United States should consult the nearest American embassy or consulate designated to act on the petition.

8. What Is the Fee?

A fee of **$545.00** must be submitted for filing this petition. However, a fee is not required for this petition if you filed an advance processing application (Form I-600A) within the previous 18 months and it was approved or is still pending.

In addition to the fee for the application, there is a **$70.00** biometric services fee for fingerprinting every adult person living in the household in the United States where the child will reside.

For example, if a petition is filed by a married people residing in the United States with one additional adult member in their household, the total fee that must be submitted would be **$755.00** (**$545.00** for the petition and **$210.00** for biometric services for fingerprinting the three adults).

NOTE: If the prospective adoptive parents and any other adult members of the household reside abroad at the time of filing, they are exempt from paying the USCIS biometric services fee. However, they may have to pay the fingerprinting fee charged by the U.S. consular office or military installation.

When more than one petition is submitted by the same petitioner on behalf of orphans who are siblings, only one Form I-600 petition and fee for biometric services is required, unless re-fingerprinting is ordered. If the orphans are not siblings, a separate filing fee must be submitted for each additional Form I-600 petition.

The fee will not be refunded, whether the petition is approved or not. **Do not mail cash.** All checks or money orders, whether U.S. or foreign, must be payable in U.S. currency at a financial institution in the United States. When a check is drawn on the account of a person other than yourself, write your name on the face of the check. If the check is not honored, USCIS will charge you $30.00.

Pay by check or money order in the exact amount. Make the check or money order payable to the **Department of Homeland Security**, unless:

A. You live in Guam, make the check or money order payable to the "Treasurer, Guam" or ;

B. You live in the U.S. Virgin Islands, make your check or money order payable to the "Commissioner of Finance of the Virgin Islands."

How to Check If the Fee Is Correct.

The fee on this form is current as of the edition date appearing in the lower right corner of this page. However, because USCIS fees change periodically, you can verify if the fee is correct by following one of the steps below:

- Visit our website at **www.uscis.gov** and scroll down to "Forms and E-Filing" to check the appropriate fee, or

- Review the Fee Schedule included in your form package, if you called us to request the form, or

- Telephone our National Customer Service Center at **1-800-375-5283** and ask for the fee information.

NOTE: If your petition or application requires a biometric services fee for USCIS to take your fingerprints, photograph or signature, you can use the same procedure above to confirm the biometrics fee.

9. Penalties.

Willful false statements on this form or supporting documents may be punished by fine or imprisonment. U.S. Code, Title 18, Sec. 1001 (formerly Sec. 80.)

10. Authority to Collect Information.

8 USC 1154(a). Routine uses for disclosure under the Privacy Act of 1974 have been published in the Federal Register and are available upon request. USCIS will use the information to determine immigrant eligibility. Submission of the information is voluntary, but failure to provide any or all of the information may result in denial of the petition.

11. USCIS Forms and Information.

To order USCIS forms, call our toll-free number at **1-800-870-3676**. You can also get USCIS forms and information on laws, regulations and procedures by telephoning our National Customer Service Center at **1-800-375-5283** or visiting our internet website at, **www.uscis.gov.**

12. Use InfoPass for Appointments.

As an alternative to waiting in line for assistance at your local USCIS office, you can now schedule an appointment through our internet-based system, **InfoPass**. To access the system, visit our website at **www.uscis.gov**. Use the **InfoPass** appointment scheduler and follow the screen prompts to set up your appointment. **InfoPass** generates an electronic appointment notice that appears on the screen. Print the notice and take it with you to your appointment. The notice gives the time and date of your appointment, along with the address of the USCIS office.

13. Reporting Burden.

A person is not required to respond to a collection of information unless it displays a currently valid OMB control number.

Public reporting burden for this collection of information is estimated to average 30 minutes per response, including the time for reviewing instructions, searching existing data sources, gathering and maintaining the data needed, and completing and reviewing the collection of information.

Send comments regarding this burden estimate or any other aspect of this collection of information, including suggestions for reducing this burden, to the: U.S. Citizenship and Immigration Services, Regulatory Management Division, 111 Massachusetts Avenue, North West, Washington, DC 20529; OMB No. 1615-0028. **Do not mail your completed petition.**

OMB No. 1615-0028; Expires 08/31/08

Department of Homeland Security
U.S. Citizenship and Immigration Services

**I-600A, Application for Advance
Processing of Orphan Petition**

Do not write in this block.	For USCIS Use Only.

It has been determined that the:

☐ Married   ☐ Unmarried

prospective adoptive parent will furnish proper care to
a beneficiary orphan if admitted to the United States.

There:

☐ are   ☐ are not

preadoptive requirements in the State of the child's proposed
residence.

The following is a description of the preadoption requirements, if any,
of the State of the child's proposed residence:

Fee Stamp

DATE OF FAVORABLE
DETERMINATION

DD

DISTRICT

The preadoption requirements, if any,:
☐ have been met.   ☐ have not been met.

File number of applicant, if applicable.

Please type or print legibly in black ink.

This application is made by the named prospective adoptive parent for advance processing of an orphan petition.

BLOCK I - Information about the prospective adoptive parent.

1. My name is: (Last)   (First)   (Middle)

2. Other names used (including maiden name if appropriate):

3. I reside in the U.S. at: (C/O if appropriate)   (Apt. No.)

   (Number and Street)   (Town or City)   (State)   (Zip Code)

4. Address abroad (If any): (Number and Street)   (Apt. No.)

   (Town or City)   (Province)   (Country)

5. I was born on: *(mm/dd/yyyy)*

   In: (Town or City)   (State or Province)   (Country)

6. My telephone number is: (Include Area Code)

7. My marital status is:
   ☐ Married
   ☐ Widowed
   ☐ Divorced
   ☐ Single
       ☐ I have never been married.
       ☐ I have been previously married _____ time(s).

8. If you are now married, give the following information:

Date and place of present marriage *(mm/dd/yyyy)*

Name of present spouse (include maiden name of wife)

Date of birth of spouse *(mm/dd/yyyy)*   Place of birth of spouse

Number of prior marriages of spouse

My spouse resides   ☐ With me   ☐ Apart from me
(provide address below)

(Apt. No.)   (No. and Street)   (City)   (State)   (Country)

9. I am a citizen of the United States through:
   ☐ Birth   ☐ Parents   ☐ Naturalization

If acquired through naturalization, give name under which naturalized,
number of naturalization certificate, and date and place of naturalization.

If not, submit evidence of citizenship. See Instruction 2.a(2).

If acquired through parentage, have you obtained a certificate in your
own name based on that acquisition?
   ☐ No   ☐ Yes

Have you or any person through whom you claimed citizenship ever lost
United States citizenship?
   ☐ No   ☐ Yes (If Yes, attach detailed explanation.)

Received	Trans. In	Ret'd Trans. Out	Completed

220

BLOCK II - General information.

10. Name and address of organization or individual assisting you in locating or identifying an orphan

(Name)

_____

(Address)

_____

11. Do you plan to travel abroad to locate or adopt a child?

☐ Yes   ☐ No

12. Does your spouse, if any, plan to travel abroad to locate or adopt a child?

☐ Yes   ☐ No

13. If the answer to Question 11 or 12 is "Yes," give the following information:

   a. Your date of intended departure _____

   b. Your spouse's date of intended departure _____

   c. City, province _____

14. Will the child come to the United States for adoption after compliance with the preadoption requirements, if any, of the State of proposed residence?

☐ Yes   ☐ No

15. If the answer to Question 14 is "No," will the child be adopted abroad after having been personally seen and observed by you and your spouse, if married?

☐ Yes   ☐ No

16. Where do you wish to file your orphan petition?

The USCIS office located at _____

The American Embassy or Consulate at _____

17. Do you plan to adopt more than one child?

☐ Yes   ☐ No

If "Yes," how many children do you plan to adopt? _____

Certification of prospective adoptive parent.

I certify, under penalty of perjury under the laws of the United States of America, that the foregoing is true and correct and that I will care for an orphan/orphans properly if admitted to the United States.

_____
(Signature of Prospective Adoptive Parent)

_____
Executed on (Date)

Certification of married prospective adoptive parent spouse.

I certify, under penalty of perjury under the laws of the United States of America, that the foregoing is true and correct and that my spouse and I will care for an orphan/orphans properly if admitted to the United States.

_____
(Signature of Prospective Adoptive Parent Spouse)

_____
Executed on (Date)

Signature of person preparing form, if other than petitioner.

I declare that this document was prepared by me at the request of the petitioner and is based entirely on information of which I have knowledge.

_____
(Signature)

_____
Street Address and Room or Suite No./City/State/Zip Code

_____
Executed on (Date)

OMB No. 1615-0028; Expires 08/31/08

Department of Homeland Security
U.S. Citizenship and Immigration Services

I-600A, Application for Advance Processing of Orphan Petition

Instructions

What Is the Purpose of This Form?

This form is used by a U.S. citizen who plans to adopt a foreign-born orphan but does not have a specific child in mind. "Advance Processing" enables USCIS to first adjudicate the application that relates to the qualifications of the applicant(s) as a prospective adoptive parent(s).

Additionally, this form may be used in cases where the child is known and the prospective adoptive parent(s) are traveling to the country where the child is located. However, it is important that prospective adoptive parent(s) be aware that the child must remain in the foreign country where he or she is located until the processing is completed.

NOTE: This Form I-600A application is not a petition to classify an orphan as an immediate relative. Form I-600, Petition to Classify Orphan as an Immediate Relative, is used for that purpose.

1. What Are the Eligibility Requirements?

A. Eligibility for advance processing application (Form I-600A).

An application for advance processing may be filed by a married U.S. citizen and spouse. The spouse of the applicant does not need to be a U.S. citizen; however, he or she must be in a lawful immigration status. An application for advance processing may also be filed by an unmarried U.S citizen who is at least 24 years of age provided that he or she will be at least 25 at the time of adoption and the filing of an orphan petition on behalf of a child.

B. Eligibility for orphan petition (Form I-600).

In addition to the requirements concerning the citizenship and age of the applicant described above in Instruction **1. A.** when a child is located and identified the following eligibility requirements will apply:

(1) Child.

Under U.S. immigration law, an orphan is an alien child who has no parents because of the death or disappearance of, abandonment or desertion by, or separation or loss from both parents.

An orphan is also a child who has only one parent who is not capable of taking care of the orphan and who has, in writing, irrevocably released the orphan for emigration and adoption.

A petition to classify an alien as an orphan (Form I-600) may not be filed on behalf of a child who is present in the United States, unless that child is in parole status and has not been adopted in the United States.

The petition must be filed before the child's 16th birthday.

(2) Adoption abroad.

If the orphan was adopted abroad, it must be established that both the married applicant and spouse or the unmarried applicant personally saw and observed the child prior to or during the adoption proceedings. The adoption decree must show that a married prospective adoptive parent and spouse adopted the child jointly or that an unmarried prospective parent was at least 25 years of age at the time of the adoption and filing of Form I-600.

(3) Proxy adoption abroad.

If both the applicant and spouse or the unmarried applicant did not personally see and observe the child prior to or during the adoption proceedings abroad the applicant (and spouse, if married) must submit a statement indicating the applicant's (and, if married the spouse's) willingness and intent to readopt the child in the United States. If requested, the applicant must submit a statement by an official of the state in which the child will reside that readoption is permissible in that State. In addition, evidence must be submitted to show compliance with the preadoption requirements, if any, of that State.

(4) Preadoption requirements.

If the orphan has not been adopted abroad, the applicant and spouse or the unmarried applicant must establish that the child will be adopted in the United States by the prospective applicant and spouse jointly or by the unmarried prospective applicant, and that the preadoption requirements, if any, of the State of the orphan's proposed residence have been met.

2. What Are the Requirements to File?

A. Proof of U. S. citizenship of the prospective adoptive parent(s).

(1) If a U.S. citizen by birth in the United States, submit a copy of the birth certificate issued by the civil registrar, vital statistics office or other civil authority. If a birth certificate is not available, submit a statement from the appropriate civil authority certifying that a birth certificate is not available. In such a situation secondary evidence must be submitted, including:

- **Church records** bearing the seal of the church showing the baptism, dedication or comparable rite occurred within two months after birth and showing the date and place of the prospective adoptive parent's birth, date of the religious ceremony and the names of the parents;

- School Records issued by the authority (preferably the first school attended) showing the date of admission to the school, prospective adoptive parent's date of birth or age at the time, the place of birth and the names of the parents;

- **Census records** (state or federal) showing the name place of birth, date of birth or age of the prospective adoptive parent listed;

- **Affidavits** sworn to or affirmed by two persons who were living at the time and who have personal knowledge of the date and place of birth in the United States of the prospective adoptive parent. Each affidavit should contain the following information regarding the person making the affidavit: his or her full name, address, date and place of birth and relationship to the prospective adoptive parent, if any and full information concerning the event and complete details of how the affiant acquired knowledge of the birth; or

- An unexpired **U.S. passport**, initially issued for ten years, may also be submitted as proof of U.S citizenship.

(2) If the prospective adoptive parent was born outside the United States, submit a copy of one of the following:

- Certificate of Naturalization or Certificate of Citizenship issued the by U.S. Citizenship and Immigration Services (USCIS) or the former Immigration and Naturalization Service (INS);

- Form FS-240, Report of Birth Abroad of a Citizen of the United States, issued by an American embassy;

- An unexpired U.S. passport initially issued for ten years; or

- An original statement from a U.S. consular officer verifying the applicant's U.S. citizenship with a valid passport.

   NOTE: Proof of the lawful immigration status of the applicant's spouse, if applicable, must be submitted. If the spouse is not a U.S. citizen, proof of her or his lawful immigration status, such as Form I-551, Permanent Resident Card; Form I-94, Arrival-Departure Record; or a copy of the biographic pages of the spouse's passport and the nonimmigrant visa pages showing an admission stamp must be submitted.

B. Proof of marriage of applicant and spouse.

The married applicant must submit a copy of the certificate of marriage and proof of termination of all prior marriages of himself or herself and spouse. In the case of an unmarried applicant who was previously married, submit proof of termination of all prior marriages.

NOTE: If any change occurs in the applicant'(s) marital status while the application is pending, immediately notify the USCIS office where the application was filed.

C. Home Study.

The home study must include a statement or attachment recommending or approving the adoption or proposed adoption, and be signed by an official of the responsible State agency in the State of the proposed residence or of an agency authorized by that State.

In the case of a child adopted abroad, the statement or attachment must be signed by an official of an appropriate public or private adoption agency which is licensed in the U.S.

The home study must be prepared by an entity (individual or organization) licensed or otherwise authorized under the laws of the State of the orphan's proposed residence to conduct research and preparation for a home study, including the required personal interviews.

If the recommending agency is licensed, the recommendation must specify that it is licensed, the State in which it is licensed, its license number, if any, and the period of validity of the license.

However, the research, including the interview and the preparation of the home study may be done by an individual or group in the United States or abroad that is satisfactory to the recommending entity.

A responsible State agency or licensed agency may accept a home study made by an unlicensed or foreign agency and use that home study as a basis for a favorable recommendation.

The home study must provide an assessment of the capabilities of the prospective adoptive parent(s) to properly parent the orphan and must include a discussion of the following areas:

(1) An assessment of the financial ability of the adoptive or prospective adoptive parents or parent.

(2) A detailed description of the accommodations where the adoptive or prospective adoptive parents or parent currently reside(s).

(3) If the prospective adoptive parent or parents residing abroad at the time of the home study, a description of the living accommodations where the child will reside in the United States, with the prospective adoptive parent or parents, if known.

(4) An assessment of the physical, mental and emotional capabilities of the adoptive or prospective adoptive parent or parents in relation to rearing and educating the child.

(5) An explanation regarding any history of abuse or violence or any complaints, charges, arrests, citations convictions, prison terms, pardons, rehabilitation decrees for breaking or violating any law or ordinance by the prospective adoptive parent(s) or any additional adult member of the household over age 18 years.

   NOTE: Having committed any crime of moral turpitude or a drug-related offense does not necessarily mean that the prospective adoptive parent(s) will be found not qualified to adopt an orphan. However, failure to disclose such information may result in denial of this application and/or any subsequent petition for an orphan.

D. Biometric services.

As part of the USCIS biometric services requirement, the following persons must be fingerprinted in connection with this application:

- The married prospective adoptive parent and spouse, if applicable, and

- Each additional adult member 18 years of age or older, of the prospective adoptive parent(s)' household. **NOTE:** Submit a copy of the birth certificate of each qualifying household member over 18.

If necessary, USCIS may also take each person's photograph and signature as part of the biometric services.

(1) Petitioners residing in the United States. After filing this petition, USCIS will notify each person in writing of the time and location where they must go to be fingerprinted. Failure to appear to be fingerprinted or for other biometric services may result in denial of this application.

(2) Petitioners residing abroad. Completed fingerprint cards (Forms FD-258) must be submitted with this application. Do not bend, fold or crease the completed fingerprint cards. The fingerprint cards must be prepared by a U.S. embassy or consulate, USCIS office or U.S. military installation.

3. General Filing Instructions.

A. Type or print legibly in black ink.

B. If extra space is needed to complete any item, attach a continuation sheet, indicate the item number, and date and sign each sheet.

C. Translations.

Any foreign language document must be accompanied by a full English translation that the translator has certified as complete and correct. The translator must also certify that he or she is competent to translate the foreign language into English.

D. Copies.

If these instructions tell you to submit a copy of document, you do not have to send the original document. However, if there are stamps, remarks, notations, etc., on the back of the original documents, also submit copies of the back of each document(s). You will not have to submit the original document unless USCIS requests it.

There are times when USCIS must request an original copy of a document. In that case, the original document is generally returned after it has been reviewed.

E. Certification.

The "Certification of Prospective Adoptive Parent" block of Form I-600A must be executed by the prospective adoptive parent. The spouse, if applicable, must execute the **"Certification of Married Prospective Adoptive Parent Spouse"** block on **Page 2** of the form. Failure to do so will result in the rejection of the Form I-600A.

F. Submission of the Application.

A prospective adoptive parent residing in the United States should send the completed application to the USCIS office having jurisdiction over his or her place of residence. A prospective adoptive parent residing outside the United States should consult the nearest American consulate for the overseas or stateside USCIS office designated to act on the application.

4. What Is the Fee.

A fee of **$545.00** must be submitted for filing this application.

In addition to the fee for the application, there is a **$70.00** biometric services fee for fingerprinting every adult person living in the household in the United States where the child will reside.

For example, if an application is filed by a married couple residing in the United States with one additional adult member in their household, the total fees that must be submitted would be **$755.00** (**$545.00** for the petition and **$210.00** for the biometric services fees for fingerprinting the three adults).

NOTE: If the prospective adoptive parent(s) and any other adult members of the household are residing abroad at the time of filing, they are exempt from paying the biometric services fee for fingerprinting. However, they may have to pay fingerprinting fees charged by the U.S. Department of State or military installation.

The fee will not be refunded, whether the application is approved or not. Do not mail cash. All checks or money orders, whether U.S. or foreign, must be payable in U.S.currency at a financial institution in the United States.When a check is drawn on the account of a person other than yourself, write your name on the face of the check. If the check is not honored, USCIS will charge you $30.00.

Pay by check or money order in the exact amount. Make the check or money order payable to the **Department of Homeland Security**, unless:

A. You live in Guam, make the check or money order payable to the "Treasurer, Guam" or

B. You live in the U.S. Virgin Islands, make your check or money order payable to the "Commissioner of Finance of the Virgin Islands."

How to Check If the Fee Is Correct.

The fee on this form is current as of the edition date appearing in the lower right corner of this page. However, because USCIS fees change periodically, you can verify if the fee is correct by following one of the steps below:

- Visit our website at **www.uscis.gov** and scroll down to "Forms and E-Filing" to check the appropriate fee, or

- Review the Fee Schedule included in your form package, if you called us to request the form, or

- Telephone our National Customer Service Center at **1-800-375-5283** and ask for the fee information.

NOTE: If your petition or application requires a biometric services fee for USCIS to take your fingerprints, photograph or signature, you can use the same procedure above to confirm the biometrics fee.

5. What Should You Do After Locating and/or Identifying a Child or Children?

Form I-600, Petition to Classify Orphan as an Immediate Relative, is filed when a child has been located and/or identified for the prospective adoptive parent(s). A new fee is not required if Form I-600 is filed within 18 months from the approval date of the Form I-600A application. If approved in the home study for more than one orphan, the prospective adoptive parent(s) may file a petition for each of the additional children to the maximum number approved. If the orphans are siblings, no additional filing fee is required. However, if the orphans are not siblings, an additional filing fee is required for each orphan beyond the first orphan.

NOTE: Approval of an advance processing application does not guarantee that the orphan petition(s) will be approved.

Form I-600 must be accompanied by all the evidence required by the instructions of that form, except where provided previously with Form I-600A.

Generally, Form I-600 should be submitted at the USCIS office where the advance processing application, Form I-600A, was filed. Prospective adoptive parent(s) going abroad to adopt or locate a child may file Form I-600 with either the USCIS office or American consulate or embassy having jurisdiction over the place where the child is residing or will be located, unless the case is being retained at the USCIS office stateside.

USCIS has offices in the following countries: Austria, China, Cuba, the Dominican Republic, El Salvador, Germany, Ghana, Great Britain, Greece, Guatemala, Haiti, Honduras, India, Italy, Jamaica, Kenya, Korea, Mexico, Pakistan, Panama, Peru, the Philippines, Russia, South Africa, Thailand and Vietnam.

6. Penalties.

Willful false statements on this form or supporting documents may be punished by fine or imprisonment. U. S. Code, Title 18, Sec. 1001 (Formerly Sec. 80.)

7. Authority for Collecting Information.

8 U.S.C 1154 (a). Routine uses for disclosure under the Privacy Act of 1974 have been published in the Federal Register and are available upon request. USCIS will use the information to determine immigrant eligibility Submission of the information is voluntary, but failure to provide any or all of the information may result in denial of the application.

8. USCIS Forms and Information.

To order USCIS forms, call our toll-free number at **1-800-870-3676**. You can also get USCIS forms and information on laws, regulations and procedures by telephoning our **National Customer Service Center** at **1-800-375-5283** or visiting our internet website at **www. uscis.gov.**

9. Use InfoPass for Appointments.

As an alternative to waiting in line for assistance at your local USCIS office, you can now schedule an appointment through our internet-based system, **InfoPass**. To access the system, visit our website at **www.uscis.gov**. Use the **InfoPass** appointment scheduler and follow the screen prompts to set up your appointment. **InfoPass** generates an electronic appointment notice that appears on the screen. Print the notice and take it with you to your appointment. The notice gives the time and date of your appointment, along with the address of the USCIS office.

10. Reporting Burden.

A person is not required to respond to a collection of information unless it displays a currently valid OMB control number. Public reporting burden for this collection of information is estimated to average 30 minutes per response including the time for reviewing instructions, searching existing data sources, gathering and maintaining the data needed, and completing and reviewing the collection of information. Send comments regarding this burden estimate or any other aspect of this collection of information, including suggestions for reducing this burden, to U.S. Citizenship and Immigration Services, Regulatory Management Division, 111 Massachusetts Avenue, N.W., Washington, DC 20529; OMB No. 1615-0028 **Do not mail your completed application to this address.**

OMB No. 1615-0075; Expires 09/30/06

I-864, Affidavit of Support
Under Section 213A of the Act

Department of Homeland Security
U.S. Citizenship and Immigration Services

Part 1. Basis for filing Affidavit of Support.

1. I, _____ ,

am the sponsor submitting this affidavit of support because (Check only one box):

a. ☐ I am the petitioner. I filed or am filing for the immigration of my relative.

b. ☐ I filed an alien worker petition on behalf of the intending immigrant, who is related to me as my _____

c. ☐ I have an ownership interest of at least 5 percent in _____ , which filed an alien worker petition on behalf of the intending immigrant, who is related to me as my _____

d. ☐ I am the only joint sponsor.

e. ☐ I am the ☐ first ☐ second of two joint sponsors. *(Check appropriate box.)*

f. ☐ The original petitioner is deceased. I am the substitute sponsor. I am the intending immigrant's _____ .

For Government Use Only
This I-864 is from:
☐ the Petitioner
☐ a Joint Sponsor #
☐ the Substitute Sponsor
☐ 5% Owner
This I-864:
☐ does not meet the requirements of section 213A.
☐ meets the requirements of section 213A.
Reviewer
Location
Date *(mm/dd/yyyy)*
Number of Affidavits of Support in file:
☐ 1   ☐ 2

Part 2. Information on the principal immigrant.

2. Last Name _____

First Name _____ Middle Name _____

3. Mailing Address Street Number and Name *(Include Apartment Number)*

City _____ State/Province _____ Zip/Postal Code _____ Country _____

4. Country of Citizenship _____ **5.** Date of Birth *(mm/dd/yyyy)* _____

6. Alien Registration Number *(if any)* A- _____ **7.** U.S. Social Security Number *(if any)* _____

Part 3. Information on the immigrant(s) you are sponsoring.

8. ☐ I am sponsoring the principal immigrant named in Part 2 above.

☐ Yes ☐ No (Applicable only in cases with two joint sponsors)

9. ☐ I am sponsoring the following family members immigrating at the same time or within six months of the principal immigrant named in **Part 2** above. Do not include any relative listed on a separate visa petition.

Name	Relationship to Sponsored Immigrant	Date of Birth *(mm/dd/yyyy)*	A-Number *(if any)*	U.S.Social Security Number *(if any)*
a.				
b.				
c.				
d.				
e.				

10. Enter the total number of immigrants you are sponsoring on this form from **Part 3**, Items **8** and **9**. ☐☐

Form I-864 (Rev. 01/15/06)N

226

Part 4. Information on the Sponsor.

11. Name	Last Name		For Government Use Only
	First Name	Middle Name	

12. Mailing Address	Street Number and Name *(Include Apartment Number)*		
	City	State or Province	
	Country	Zip/Postal Code	

13. Place of Residence *(if different from mailing address)*	Street Number and Name *(Include Apartment Number)*		
	City	State or Province	
	Country	Zip/Postal Code	

14. Telephone Number *(Include Area Code or Country and City Codes)*

15. Country of Domicile

16. Date of Birth *(mm/dd/yyyy)*

17. Place of Birth *(City)*	State or Province	Country

18. U.S. Social Security Number *(Required)*

19. Citizenship/Residency

☐ I am a U.S. citizen.

☐ I am a U.S. national (for joint sponsors only).

☐ I am a lawful permanent resident. My alien registration number is A-

If you checked box (b), (c), (d), (e) or (f) in line 1 on Page 1, you must include proof of your citizen, national, or permanent resident status.

20. Military Service (To be completed by petitioner sponsors only.)

I am currently on active duty in the U.S. armed services.   ☐ Yes   ☐ No

Part 5. Sponsor's household size.

	For Government Use Only

21. Your Household Size - <u>DO NOT COUNT ANYONE TWICE</u>

Persons you are sponsoring in this affidavit:

　　a. Enter the number you entered on line 10.　　□□

Persons NOT sponsored in this affidavit:

　　b. Yourself.　　**1**

　　c. If you are currently married, enter "1" for your spouse.　　□

　　d. If you have dependent children, enter the number here.　　□□

　　e. If you have any other dependents, enter the number here.　　□□

　　f. If you have sponsored any other persons on an I-864 or I-864 EZ who are now lawful permanent residents, enter the number here.　　□□

　　g. OPTIONAL: If you have <u>siblings, parents, or adult children</u> with the same principal residence who are combining their income with yours by submitting Form I-864A, enter the number here.　　□□

　　h. Add together lines and enter the number here. **Household Size:**　　□□

Part 6. Sponsor's income and employment.

22. I am currently:

　a. ☐ Employed as a/an _____ .

　　　Name of Employer #1 *(if applicable)* _____ .

　　　Name of Employer #2 *(if applicable)* _____ .

　b. ☐ Self-employed as a/an _____ .

　c. ☐ Retired from _____ since _____ .
　　　　　　　　　(Company Name)　　　　　　*(Date)*

　d. ☐ Unemployed since _____ .
　　　　　　　　　　　　　　(Date)

23. My current individual annual income is:　　$ _____
　　　　　　　　　　　　　　　　　　　(See Step-by-Step Instructions)

228

24. My current annual household income:

a. **List your income from line 23 of this form.** $ _____

b. **Income you are using from any other person who was counted in your household size,** including, in certain conditions, the intending immigrant. (See step-by-step instructions.) Please indicate name, relationship and income.

Name	Relationship	Current Income
_____	_____	$ _____
_____	_____	$ _____
_____	_____	$ _____
_____	_____	$ _____

c. **Total Household Income:** $ _____

(Total all lines from 24a and 24b. Will be Compared to Poverty Guidelines -- See Form I-864P.)

d. ☐ The persons listed above have completed Form I-864A. I am filing along with this form all necessary Forms I-864A completed by these persons.

e. ☐ The person listed above, _____ does not need to

(Name)

complete Form I-864A because he/she is the intending immigrant and has no accompanying dependents.

25. Federal income tax return information.

☐ I have filed a Federal tax return for each of the three most recent tax years. I have attached the required photocopy or transcript of my Federal tax return for only the most recent tax year.

My total income (adjusted gross income on IRS Form 1040EZ) as reported on my Federal tax returns for the most recent three years was:

Tax Year		Total Income
_____	*(most recent)*	$ _____
_____	*(2nd most recent)*	$ _____
_____	*(3rd most recent)*	$ _____

☐ *(Optional)* I have attached photocopies or transcripts of my Federal tax returns for my second and third most recent tax years.

For Government Use Only

Household Size =

_____

Poverty line for year

_____ is:

$ _____

Part 7. Use of assets to supplement income. *(Optional)*

	For Government Use Only

If your income, or the total income for you and your household, from line 24c exceeds the Federal Poverty Guidelines for your household size, YOU ARE NOT REQUIRED to complete this Part. Skip to Part 8.

Household Size =

_____

26. Your assets *(Optional)*

   a. Enter the balance of all savings and checking accounts. $ _____

Poverty line for year

_____ **is:**

   b. Enter the net cash value of real-estate holdings. (Net means current assessed value minus mortgage debt.) $ _____

$ _____

   c. Enter the net cash value of all stocks, bonds, certificates of deposit, and any other assets not already included in lines 26 (a) or (b). $ _____

   d. Add together lines 26 a, b and c and enter the number here.   **TOTAL:** $ _____

27. Your household member's assets from Form I-864A. *(Optional)*

Assets from Form I-864A, line 12d for

_____ $ _____

(Name of Relative)

28. Assets of the principal sponsored immigrant. *(Optional)*

The principal sponsored immigrant is the person listed in line 2.

   a. Enter the balance of the sponsored immigrant's savings and checking accounts. $ _____

   b. Enter the net cash value of all the sponsored immigrant's real estate holdings. (Net means investment value minus mortgage debt.) $ _____

   c. Enter the current cash value of the sponsored immigrant's stocks, bonds, certificates of deposit, and other assets not included on line a or b. $ _____

   d. Add together lines 28a, b, and c, and enter the number here. $ _____

The total value of all assets, line 29, must equal 5 times (3 times for spouses and children of USCs, or 1 time for orphans to be formally adopted in the U.S.) the difference between the poverty guidelines and the sponsor's household income, line 24c.

29. Total value of assets.

Add together lines 26d, 27 and 28d and enter the number here.   **TOTAL:** $ _____

Part 8. Sponsor's Contract.

Please note that, by signing this Form I-864, you agree to assume certain specific obligations under the Immigration and Nationality Act and other Federal laws. The following paragraphs describe those obligations. Please read the following information carefully before you sign the Form I-864. If you do not understand the obligations, you may wish to consult an attorney or accredited representative.

What is the Legal Effect of My Signing a Form I-864?

If you sign a Form I-864 on behalf of any person (called the "intending immigrant") who is applying for an immigrant visa or for adjustment of status to a permanent resident, and that intending immigrant submits the Form I-864 to the U.S. Government with his or her application for an immigrant visa or adjustment of status, under section 213A of the Immigration and Nationality Act these actions create a contract between you and the U. S. Government. The intending immigrant's becoming a permanent resident is the "consideration" for the contract.

Under this contract, you agree that, in deciding whether the intending immigrant can establish that he or she is not inadmissible to the United States as an alien likely to become a public charge, the U.S. Government can consider your income and assets to be available for the support of the intending immigrant.

What If I choose Not to Sign a Form I-864?

You cannot be made to sign a Form I-864 if you do not want to do so. But if you do not sign the Form I-864, the intending immigrant may not be able to become a permanent resident in the United States.

What Does Signing the Form I-864 Require Me to do?

If an intending immigrant becomes a permanent resident in the United States based on a Form I-864 that you have signed, then, until your obligations under the Form I-864 terminate, you must:

-- Provide the intending immigrant any support necessary to maintain him or her at an income that is at least 125 percent of the Federal Poverty Guidelines for his or her household size (100 percent if you are the petitioning sponsor and are on active duty in the U.S. Armed Forces and the person is your husband, wife, unmarried child under 21 years old.)

-- Notify USCIS of any change in your address, within 30 days of the change, by filing Form I-865.

What Other Consequences Are There?

If an intending immigrant becomes a permanent resident in the United States based on a Form I-864 that you have signed, then until your obligations under the Form I-864 terminate, your income and assets may be considered ("deemed") to be available to that person, in determining whether he or she is eligible for certain Federal means-tested public benefits and also for State or local means-tested public benefits, if the State or local government's rules provide for consideration ("deeming") of your income and assets as available to the person.

This provision does **not** apply to public benefits specified in section 403(c) of the Welfare Reform Act such as, but not limited to, emergency Medicaid, short-term, non-cash emergency relief; services provided under the National School Lunch and Child Nutrition Acts; immunizations and testing and treatment for communicable diseases; and means-tested programs under the Elementary and Secondary Education Act.

Contract continued on following page.

What If I Do Not Fulfill My Obligations?

If you do not provide sufficient support to the person who becomes a permanent resident based on the Form I-864 that you signed, that person may sue you for this support.

If a Federal, State or local agency, or a private agency, provides any covered means-tested public benefit to the person who becomes a permanent resident based on the Form I-864 that you signed, the agency may ask you to reimburse them for the amount of the benefits they provided. If you do not make the reimbursement, the agency may sue you for the amount that the agency believes you owe.

If you are sued, and the court enters a judgment against you, the person or agency that sued you may use any legally permitted procedures for enforcing or collecting the judgment. You may also be required to pay the costs of collection, including attorney fees.

If you do not file a properly completed Form I-865 within 30 days of any change of address, USCIS may impose a civil fine for your failing to do so.

When Will These Obligations End?

Your obligations under a Form I-864 will end if the person who becomes a permanent resident based on a Form I-864 that you signed:

- Becomes a U.S. citizen;
- Has worked, or can be credited with, 40 quarters of coverage under the Social Security Act;
- No longer has lawful permanent resident status, and has departed the United States;
- Becomes subject to removal, but applies for and obtains in removal proceedings a new grant of adjustment of status, based on a new affidavit of support, if one is required; or
- Dies.

Note that divorce **does not** terminate your obligations under this Form I-864.

Your obligations under a Form I-864 also end if you die. Therefore, if you die, your Estate will not be required to take responsibility for the person's support after your death. Your Estate may, however, be responsible for any support that you owed before you died.

30. I, _____ .
                                                         (Print Sponsor's Name)

certify under penalty of perjury under the laws of the United States that:

a.   I know the contents of this affidavit of support that I signed.

b.   All the factual statements in this affidavit of support are true and correct.

c.   I have read and I understand each of the obligations described in Part 8, and I agree, freely and without any mental reservation or purpose of evasion, to accept each of those obligations in order to make it possible for the immigrants indicated in Part 3 to become permanent residents of the United States;

d.   I agree to submit to the personal jurisdiction of any Federal or State court that has subject matter jurisdiction of a lawsuit against me to enforce my obligations under this Form I-864;

e.   Each of the Federal income tax returns submitted in support of this affidavit are true copies, or are unaltered tax transcripts, of the tax returns I filed with the U.S. Internal Revenue Service; and

Sign on following page.

f. I authorize the Social Security Administration to release information about me in its records to the Department of State and U.S. Citizenship and Immigration Services.

g. Any and all other evidence submitted is true and correct.

31. _____   _____
                  (Sponsor's Signature)   *(Date-- mm/dd/yyyy)*

Part 9. Information on Preparer, if prepared by someone other than the sponsor.

I certify under penalty of perjury under the laws of the United States that I prepared this affidavit of support at the sponsor's request and that this affidavit of support is based on all information of which I have knowledge.

Signature: _____   **Date:** _____
                                                                      (mm/dd/yyyy)

Printed Name: _____

Firm Name: _____

Address: _____

Telephone Number: _____

E-Mail Address : _____

Business State ID # *(if any)* _____

OMB No. 1615-0075; Expires 09/30/06

Department of Homeland Security
U.S. Citizenship and Immigration Services

I-864, Affidavit of Support
Under Section 213A of the Act

Instructions

How Should I Complete This Form?

- Print clearly or type your answers using CAPITAL letters.

- Use black or blue ink.

- If you need extra space to answer any item:

  -- Attach a separate sheet of paper (or more sheets if necessary);

  -- Write your name, U.S. Social Security number and the words "Form I-864" on the top right corner of the sheet; and

  -- Write the number and subject of each question for which you are providing additional information.

What Is the Purpose of This Form?

This form is required for most family-based immigrants and some employment-based immigrants to show that they have adequate means of financial support and that they are not likely to become a public charge. For more information about Form I-864, or to obtain related forms please contact:

- The USCIS website (**www.uscis.gov**);

- The National Customer Service Center (NCSC) telephone line at 1-800-375-5283 TTY: (1-800-767-1833); or

- Your local USCIS office by using Infopass.

How Is This Form Used?

This form is a contract between a sponsor and the U.S. Government. Completing and signing this form makes you the sponsor. You must show on this form that you have enough income and/or assets to maintain the intending immigrant(s) and the rest of your household at 125 percent of the Federal Poverty Guidelines. By signing Form I-864, you are agreeing to use your resources to support the intending immigrant(s) named in this form, if it becomes necessary.

The submission of this form may make the sponsored immigrant ineligible for certain Federal, State, or local means-tested public benefits, because an agency that provides means-tested public benefits will consider *your* resources and assets as available to the sponsored immigrant in determining his or her eligibility for the program.

If the immigrant sponsored in this affidavit does receive one of the designated Federal, State or local means-tested public benefits, the agency providing the benefit may request that you repay the cost of those benefits. That agency can sue you if the cost of the benefits provided is not repaid.

Not all benefits are considered to be means-tested public benefits. See Form I-864P, Poverty Guidelines, for more information on which benefits may be covered by this definition, or the contract on **Page 6** of this form for a list of benefits explicitly not considered means-tested public benefits.

Who Needs This Form?

The following immigrants are required by law to submit Form I-864 completed by the petitioner to obtain an immigrant visa overseas or to adjust status to that of a lawful permanent resident in the United States:

- All immediate relatives of U.S. citizens (spouses, unmarried children under age 21, and parents of U.S. citizens age 21 and older);

- All family-based preference immigrants (unmarried sons and daughters of U.S. citizens, spouses and unmarried sons and daughters of permanent resident aliens, married sons and daughters of U.S. citizens, and brothers and sisters of U.S. citizens age 21 and older); and

- Employment-based preference immigrants in cases only when a U.S. citizen or lawful permanent resident relative filed the immigrant visa petition or such relative has a significant ownership interest (five percent or more) in the entity that filed the petition.

Are There Exceptions to Who Needs This Form?

The following types of intending immigrants do not need to file this form:

- Any intending immigrant who has earned or can be credited with 40 qualifying quarters (credits) of work in the United States. In addition to their own work, intending immigrants may be able to secure credit for work performed by a spouse during marriage and by their parent(s) while the immigrants were under 18 years of age. The Social Security Administration (SSA) can provide information on how to count quarters of work earned or credited and how to provide evidence of such. See the SSA website at www.ssa.gov/mystatement/credits for more information;

- Any intending immigrant who will, upon admission, acquire U.S. citizenship under section 320 of the Immigration and Nationality Act, as amended by the Child Citizenship Act of 2000 (CCA);

- Self-petitioning widow/ers who have an approved Petition for Amerasian, Widow(er), or Special Immigrant, Form I-360; and

- Self-petitioning battered spouses and children who have an approved Petition for Amerasian, Widow(er), or Special Immigrant, Form I-360.

NOTE: *If you qualify for one of the exemptions listed above, submit Form I-864W, Intending Immigrant's I-864 Exemption, instead of Form I-864.*

Who Completes and Signs Form I-864?

A sponsor completes and signs Form I-864. A sponsor is required to be at least 18 years old and domiciled in the United States, or its territories or possessions (see Step-by-step Instructions for more information on domicile). The petitioning sponsor must sign and complete Form I-864, even if a joint sponsor also submits an I-864 to meet the income requirement. The list below identifies who must become sponsors by completing and signing a Form I-864.

- The U.S. citizen or lawful permanent resident who filed a Form I-130 for a family member, Form I-129F for a fiance(e), or Form I-600 or I-600A for an orphan.

- The U.S. citizen or permanent resident alien who filed an employment-based immigrant visa petition (Form I-140) for a spouse, parent, son, daughter, or sibling who: (**1**) has a significant ownership interest (five percent or more) in the business which filed the employment-based immigrant visa petition; or (**2**) is related to the intending immigrant as a spouse, parent, son, daughter, or sibling.

What Are the Income Requirements?

To qualify as a sponsor, you must demonstrate that your income is at least 125 percent of the current Federal poverty guideline for your household size. The Federal poverty line, for purposes of this form, is updated annually and can be found on Form I-864P, Poverty Guidelines.

If you are on active duty in the U.S. Armed Forces, including the Army, Navy, Air Force, Marines or Coast Guard, and you are sponsoring your spouse or minor child, you only need to have an income of 100 percent of the Federal poverty line for your household size. This provision does not apply to joint or substitute sponsors.

How Do I Count Household Size?

Your household size includes yourself and the following individuals, no matter where they live: any spouse, any dependent children under the age of 21, any other dependents listed on your most recent Federal income tax return, all persons being sponsored in this affidavit of support, and any immigrants previously sponsored with a Form I-864 or Form I-864 EZ affidavit of support whom you are still obligated to support. If necessary to meet the income requirements to be a sponsor, you may include additional relatives (adult children, parents, or siblings) as part of your household size as long as they have the same principle residence as you and promise to use their income and resources in support of the intending immigrant(s).

What If I Cannot Meet the Income Requirements?

If your income alone is not sufficient to meet the requirement for your household size, the intending immigrant will be ineligible for an immigrant visa or adjustment of status, unless the requirement can be met using any combination of the following:

- Income from any relatives or dependents living in your household or dependents listed on your most recent Federal tax return who signed a Form I-864A;

- Income from the intending immigrant, if that income will continue from the same source after immigration, and if the intending immigrant is currently living in your residence. If the intending immigrant is your spouse, his or her income can be counted regardless of current residence, but it must continue from the same source after he or she becomes a lawful permanent resident.

- The value of your assets, the assets of any household member who has signed a Form I-864A, or the assets of the intending immigrant;

- A joint sponsor whose income and/or assets equal at least 125 percent of the Poverty Guidelines. See question below for more information on joint sponsors.

How Can My Relatives and Dependents Help Me Meet the Income Requirements?

You may use the income of your spouse and/or any other relatives living in your residence if they are willing to be jointly responsible with you for the intending immigrant(s) you are sponsoring. If you have any unrelated dependents listed on your income tax return you may include their income regardless of where they reside.

The income of such household members and dependents can be used to help you meet the income requirements if they complete and sign Form I-864A, Contract Between Sponsor and Household Member, and if they are at least 18 years of age when they sign the form.

Can the Intending Immigrant Help Me Meet the Income Requirements?

If certain conditions are met, the intending immigrant's income can help you meet the income requirement. If the intending immigrant is your spouse, his or her income can be included if it will continue from the same source after he or she obtains lawful permanent resident status. If the intending immigrant is another relative, there are two requirements.

First, the income must be continuing from the same source after he or she obtains lawful permanent resident status, and second, the intending immigrant must currently live with you in your residence. Evidence must be provided to support both requirements.

However, an intending immigrant whose income is being used to meet the income requirement does not need to complete Form I-864A, Contract Between Sponsor and Household Member, unless the intending immigrant has a spouse and/or children immigrating with him or her. In this instance, the contract relates to support for the spouse and/or children.

Does Receipt of Means-Tested Public Benefits Disqualify me From being a Sponsor?

No. Receipt of means-tested public benefits does not disqualify anyone from being a sponsor. However, means-tested public benefits cannot be accepted as income for the purposes of meeting the income requirement.

How Can I Use Assets to Qualify?

Assets may supplement income if the consular or immigration officer is convinced that the monetary value of the asset could reasonably be made available to support the sponsored immigrant and converted to cash within one year without undue harm to the sponsor or his or her family members. You may not include an automobile unless you show that you own at least one working automobile that you have not included.

What Is a Joint Sponsor?

If the person who is seeking the immigration of one or more of his or her relatives cannot meet the income requirements, a "joint sponsor" who can meet the requirements may submit a Form I-864 to sponsor all or some of the family members.

A joint sponsor can be any U.S. citizen, U.S. national, or lawful permanent resident who is at least 18 years old, domiciled in the United States, or its territories or possessions, and willing to be held jointly liable with the petitioner for the support of the intending immigrant. A joint sponsor does not have to be related to the petitioning sponsor or the intending immigrant.

If the first joint sponsor completes Form I-864 for some rather than all the family members, a second qualifying joint sponsor will be required to sponsor the remaining family members. There may be no more than two joint sponsors. A joint sponsor must be able to meet the income requirements for all the persons he or she is sponsoring without combining resources with the petitioning sponsor or a second joint sponsor. Any dependents applying for an immigrant visa or adjustment of status more than six months after immigration of the intending immigrants must be sponsored by the petitioner but may be sponsored by an original joint sponsor or a different joint sponsor.

Even if one or more I-864s are submitted for an intending immigrant, the petitioning sponsor remains legally accountable for the financial support of the sponsored alien along with the joint sponsor(s).

What Is a Substitute Sponsor?

A substitute sponsor is a sponsor who is completing a Form I-864 on behalf of an intending immigrant whose original I-130 petitioner has died after the Form I-130 was approved, but before the intending immigrant obtained permanent residence.

The substitute sponsor must be related to the intending immigrant in one of the following ways: spouse, parent, mother-in-law, father-in-law, sibling, child (at least 18 years of age), son, daughter, son-in-law, daughter-in-law, brother-in-law, sister-in-law, grandparent, grandchild or legal guardian. The substitute sponsor must also be a U.S. citizen or lawful permanent resident.

If you are a substitute sponsor, you must indicate that that you are related to the intending immigrant in one of the ways listed above and include evidence proving that relationship. The beneficiary must also file this form along with a written statement explaining the reasons why the Form I-130 visa petition should be reinstated, having been revoked following the petitioner's death. The beneficiary must also include a copy of the Form I-130 approval notice.

How Long Does My Obligation as a Sponsor Continue?

Your obligation to support the immigrant(s) you are sponsoring in this affidavit of support will continue until the sponsored immigrant becomes a U.S. citizen, or can be credited with 40 qualifying quarters of work in the United States.

Although 40 qualifying quarters of work (credits) generally equate to ten years of work, in certain cases the work of a spouse or parent adds qualifying quarters. The Social Security Administration can provide information on how to count qualifying quarters (credits) of work.

The obligation also ends if you or the sponsored immigrant dies or if the sponsored immigrant ceases to be a lawful permanent resident and departs the United States. Divorce does not end the sponsorship obligation.

Do I Need to Submit a Separate Affidavit for Each Family Member?

You must submit a Form I-864 affidavit of support for each intending immigrant you are sponsoring. You may submit photocopies if you are sponsoring more than one intending immigrant listed on the same affidavit of support.

Separate affidavits of support are required for intending immigrants for whom different Form I-130 family-based petitions were filed. For instance, if you are sponsoring both parents, each will need an original affidavit of support and accompanying documentation since you were required to submit separate Form I-130 visa petitions for each parent.

Often a spouse or minor children obtain visas or adjust status as dependents of a relative, based on the same visa petition. If you are sponsoring such dependents, you only need to provide a photocopy of the original Form I-864, as long as these dependents are immigrating at the same time as the principal immigrant or within six months of the time he or she immigrates to the United States. You do not need to provide copies of the supporting documents for each of the photocopied Forms I-864.

When Do I Complete Form I-864 and Where Do I Send It?

If the intending immigrant will apply for an immigrant visa at a U.S. Embassy or Consulate overseas:

Complete Form I-864 when it is mailed to you from the National Visa Center (NVC). Different instructions apply to some cases so follow the instructions provided by the National Visa Center for your particular case. The instructions on when and where to submit Form I-864 are included in the information packet that is mailed to you with Form I-864. Form I-864 and all accompanying documentation must be submitted to the government within one year of when you sign Form I-864.

If the intending immigrant will adjust status in the United States:

Complete Form I-864 when the intending immigrant is ready to submit his or her Form Application to Register Permanent Residence or Adjust Status. Then give the completed Form I-864 along with any Forms I-864A and all supporting documentation to the intending immigrant to submit with his or her application for adjustment of status. To be valid, Form I-864 and all supporting documentation must be submitted within one year of when you sign Form I-864. For privacy, you may enclose these documents in a sealed envelope marked "Form I-864: To Be Opened Only by a U.S. Government Official." You may be requested to submit updated information if there is a significant delay in processing.

Do I Have to Report My Change of Address If I Move?

Federal law requires that every sponsor report every change of address to the USCIS within 30 days of the change. To do this, send a completed Form I-865, Sponsor's Change of Address, to the Service Center having jurisdiction over your new address.

Do not complete Form I-865 at the same time that you complete the I-864.

You should complete and submit Form I-865 to USCIS only when the address you indicated on the original I-864 Affidavit of Support has changed. Please see Form I-865 for further directions on filing the Sponsor's Change of Address. This requirement does not relieve a sponsor who is a lawful permanent resident from submitting Form AR-11 within ten days of a change of address.

Step-by-Step Instructions
Form I-864 is divided into nine parts. The information below will help you fill out the form.

Part 1. Basis for Filing Affidavit of Support.

- Check **box "a"** if you are the petitioner who is filing or who has already filed Form I-130, Petition for Alien Relative; Form I-600, Petition to Classify Orphan as an Immediate Relative; or Form I-600A, Application for Advance Processing of Orphan Petition. If you are the petitioner, you must sponsor each intending immigrant.

- Check **box "b"** if you are filing or have filed Form I-140, Immigrant Petition for Alien Worker, for your husband, wife, father, mother, child, adult son or daughter, brother, or sister.

- Check **box "c"** if you have an ownership interest of at least five percent in a business, corporation or other entity that filed or is filing a Form I-140 for your husband, wife, father, mother, child, adult son or daughter, brother, or sister.

- Check **box "d"** if you are the only joint sponsor or box "e" if you are either of two joint sponsors. A joint sponsor must be a person, and may not be a corporation, organization, or other entity. A joint sponsor does not have to be related to the intending immigrant. Indicate whether you are the only joint sponsor or one of two joint sponsors. Check with the petitioning sponsor or the intending immigrant if you are not certain.

- Check **box "f"** if you are the substitute sponsor. A substitute sponsor is a sponsor who is completing a Form I-864 on behalf of an intending immigrant whose original Form I-130 petitioner has died after the Form I-130 was approved, but before the intending immigrant obtained permanent residence. The substitute sponsor must be related to the intending immigrant in one of the following ways: spouse, parent, mother-in-law, father-in-law, sibling, child (at least 18 years of age), son, daughter, son-in-law, daughter-in-law, brother-in-law, sister-in-law, grandparent, grandchild or legal guardian. The substitute sponsor must also be a U.S. citizen or lawful permanent resident. If you are a substitute sponsor, you must sponsor each intending immigrant.

Part 2. Information on the Principal Immigrant.
The principal immigrant is the intending immigrant who is the primary beneficiary of the visa petition.

6. Alien Registration Number. An "A-number" is an Alien Registration Number assigned by the former Immigration and Naturalization Service (INS) or U.S. Citizenship and Immigration Services (USCIS). If the intending immigrants you are sponsoring have not previously been in the United States or have only been in the United States as tourists, they probably do not have A-numbers. Persons with A-numbers can locate the number on their INS or USCIS-issued documentation.

8. Indicate whether you are sponsoring the principal immigrant listed in **item 2** in this Form I-864. This only applies to cases with two joint sponsors. Check "No" only if you are sponsoring only intended immigrants listed in **9** (a through e) and not the principal immigrant listed in **item 2**.

Part 3. Information on Immigrants You Are Sponsoring.

9. Accompanying Family Members You are Sponsoring The immigrant you are sponsoring may be bringing a spouse and/or children to the United States. If the spouse and/or children will be traveling with the immigrant, or within six months of the immigrant's entry to the United States and you are sponsoring them, you should list the names and other requested information on the lines provided. If any dependents are not immigrating, will be immigrating more than 6 months after the sponsored alien arrives in the United States, or you are not sponsoring them, do not list their names here. A separate Form I-864 will be required for them when they apply for their immigrant visas.

Part 4. Information on the Sponsor.

15. Country of Domicile. This question is asking you to indicate the country where you maintain your principal residence and where you plan to reside for the foreseeable future. If your mailing address and/or place of residence is not in the United States, but your country of domicile is the United States, you must attach a written explanation and documentary evidence indicating how you meet the domicile requirement. If you are not currently living in the United States, you may meet the domicile requirement if you can submit evidence to establish that any of the following conditions apply:

238

A. You are employed by a certain organization.

Some individuals employed overseas are automatically considered to be domiciled in the United States because of the nature of their employment. The qualifying types of employment include employment by:

-- The U.S. government;

-- An American institution of research recognized by the Secretary of Homeland Security (The list of qualifying institutions may be found at 8 CFR 316.20);

-- A U.S. firm or corporation engaged in whole or in part in the development of foreign trade and commerce with the United States, or a subsidiary of such a firm or corporation;

-- A public international organization in which the United States participates by treaty or statute;

-- A religious denomination having a bona fide organization in the United States, if the employment abroad involves the person's performance of priestly or ministerial functions on behalf of the denomination; or

-- A religious denomination or interdenominational missionary organization having a bona fide organization in the United States, if the person is engaged solely as a missionary.

B. You are living abroad temporarily.

If you are not currently living in the United States, you must show that your trip abroad is temporary and that you have maintained your domicile in the United States. You can show this by providing proof of your voting record in the United States, proof of paying U.S. State or local taxes, proof of having property in the United States, proof of maintaining bank or investment accounts in the United States, or proof of having a permanent mailing address in the United States. Other proof could be evidence that you are a student studying abroad or that a foreign government has authorized a temporary stay.

C. You intend in good faith to reestablish your domicile in the United States no later than the date of the intending immigrant's admission or adjustment of status.

You must submit proof that you have taken concrete steps to establish you will be domiciled in the United States at a time no later than the date of the intending immigrant's admission or adjustment of status. Concrete steps might include accepting a job in the United States, signing a lease or purchasing a residence in the United States, or registering children in U.S. schools. Please attach proof of the steps you have taken to establish domicile as described above.

18. U.S. Social Security Number.

Every sponsor's Social Security number is required by law. If you do not currently have a Social Security number you must obtain one before submitting this Form I-864.

19. Citizenship/Residency.

Proof of U.S. citizen, national, or permanent resident status is required for joint and substitute sponsors and for relatives of employment-based immigrants who file this form. Petitioning relatives who have already filed proof of their citizenship or immigration status with Forms I-130, Form I-129F, I-600 and I-600A do not need to submit proof of their status with this form.

Proof of U.S. citizen or national status includes a copy of your birth certificate, certificate of naturalization, certificate of citizenship, consular report of birth abroad to citizen parents, or a copy of the biographic data page of your U.S. passport.

Proof of permanent resident status includes a photocopy of both sides of the "green card," Form I-551, Alien Registration Receipt Card/Permanent Resident Card; or a photocopy of an unexpired temporary I-551 stamp in either a foreign passport or a DHS Form I-94, Arrival/Departure Document.

20. Military Service.

Check "yes" if you are the petitioning sponsor and on active duty in the U.S. Army, Navy, Air Force, Marines, or Coast Guard, other than for training. If you provide evidence that you are currently on active duty in the military and you are petitioning for your spouse or minor child, you will need to demonstrate income at only 100 percent of the poverty level for your household size, instead of at 125 percent of the poverty level. (See Form I-864P for information on the poverty levels.) Check "no" if you are not on active duty in the U.S. military. This provision does not apply to joint and substitute sponsors.

Part 5. Sponsor's Household Size.

This section asks you to add together the number of persons for whom you are financially responsible. Some of these persons may not be residing with you. Make sure you do not count any individual more than once, since in some cases the same person could fit into two categories. For example, your spouse (whom you would enter on **line 21c**) might also be a lawful permanent resident whom you have already sponsored using Form I-864 (**line 21f**). If you included your spouse on line 21c, do not include him or her again on **line 21f**.

21d - Enter the number of unmarried children you have who are under age 21, even if you do not have legal custody of these children. You may exclude any unmarried children under 21, if these children have reached majority under the law of their place of domicile and you do not claim them as dependents on your income tax returns.

21e - Enter the number of any other dependents. You must include each and every person whom you have claimed as a dependent on your most recent Federal income tax return, even if that person is not related to you. Even if you are not *legally obligated* to support that person, you must include the person if in fact you did support that person and claimed the person as a dependent.

21f - Enter the number of lawful permanent residents whom you are currently obligated to support based on your previous submission of Form I-864 as a petitioning, substitute, or joint sponsor, or of Form I-864EZ as a petitioning sponsor. Include only those persons who have already immigrated to the United States. Do not include anyone for whom your obligation to support has ended through the sponsored immigrant's acquisition of U.S. citizenship, death, abandonment of lawful permanent residence in the United States, acquisition of 40 quarters of earned or credited work in the United States, or obtaining a new grant of adjustment of status while in removal proceedings based on a new affidavit of support, if one is required.

21g - This question gives you the option of including certain other non-dependent relatives who are living in your residence as part of your household size. Such relatives may include your mother, father, sister, brother or adult children, if they are living in your residence. However, the only reason to include these family members in your household size is if you need to include their income when you calculate your household income for purposes of meeting the income requirement for this form. To be considered, any relative indicated in this category must sign and submit Form I-864A.

Part 6. Sponsor's Income and Employment.

22. Job Classification.

Check the box (**a through d**) that applies to you.

23. Current Individual Annual Income.

Enter your current individual earned or retirement annual income that you are using to meet the requirements of this form and indicate the total on this line.

You may include evidence supporting your claim about your expected income for the current year if you believe that submitting this evidence will help you establish ability to maintain sufficient income. **You are not required to submit this evidence, however, unless specifically instructed to do so by a Government official.** For example, you may include a recent letter from your employer, showing your employer's address and telephone number, and indicating your annual salary. You may also provide pay stub(s) showing your income for the previous six months. If your claimed income includes alimony, child support, dividend or interest income, or income from any other source, you may also include evidence of that income.

24. Annual Household Income.

This section is used to determine the sponsor's household income. Take your annual individual income from **line 23** and enter it on **line 24a**. If this amount is greater than 125 percent (or 100 percent if you are on active duty in the U.S. military and sponsoring your spouse or child) of the Federal Poverty Guidelines for your household size from **line 21h**, you do not need to include any household member's income. See Form I-864P for reference on the Poverty Guidelines.

To determine the filing requirements for your relatives included in **item 24b**, follow these instructions:

- If you included the income of your **spouse** listed in **21c**, or any **child** listed in **21d**, or any **dependent** listed in **21e**, or any **other relative** listed in **21g**, each one of these individuals must be over 18 years of age and must complete Form I-864A.

- If you included the income of the intending immigrant who is your spouse (he or she would be counted on line **21a**), evidence that his/her income will continue from the current source after obtaining lawful permanent resident status must be provided. He/she does not need to complete Form I-864A unless he/she has accompanying children.

- If you included the income of the intending immigrant who is not your spouse, (he or she would be counted on line **21a**), evidence that his or her income will continue from the current source after obtaining lawful permanent resident status must be provided **and** the intending immigrant must provide evidence that he/she is living in your residence. He or she does not need to complete Form I-864A, Contract Between Sponsor and Household Member, unless he or she has an accompanying spouse or children.

240

25. Federal Income Tax Information.

You must provide either an IRS transcript or a photocopy from your own records of your Federal individual income tax return for the most recent tax year. If you believe additional returns may help you to establish your ability to maintain sufficient income, you may submit transcripts or photocopies of your Federal individual income tax returns for the three most recent years.

You are not required to have the IRS certify the transcript or photocopy unless specifically instructed to do so by a Government official; a plain transcript or photocopy is acceptable. Telefile tax records are not acceptable proof of filing.

Do not submit copies of your State income tax returns. **Do not** submit any tax returns that you filed with any foreign government unless you claim that you were not required to file a Federal tax return with the United States government and you wish to rely on the foreign return solely to establish the amount of your income that is not subject to tax in the United States.

If you provide a photocopy of your tax return(s), you must include a copy of each and every Form W-2 and Form 1099 that relates to your return(s). Do not include copies of these Forms if you provide an IRS transcript of your return(s) rather than a photocopy.

If you checked box **22(b)** (self-employed), you should have completed one of the following forms with your Federal income tax return: Schedule C (Profit or Loss from Business), Schedule D (Capital Gains), Schedule E (Supplemental Income or Loss) or Schedule F (Profit or Loss from Farming). You must include each and every Form 1040 Schedule, if any, that you filed with your Federal tax return.

If you were required to file a Federal income tax return during any of the previous three tax years but did not do so, you must file any and all late returns with IRS and attach an IRS-generated tax return transcript documenting your late filing before submitting the I-864 Affidavit of Support. If you were not required to file a Federal income tax return under U.S. tax law because your income was too low, attach a written explanation. If you were not required to file a Federal income tax return under U.S. tax law for any other reason, attach a written explanation including evidence of the exemption and how you are subject to it. Residence outside of the United States does not exempt U.S. citizens or lawful permanent

residents from filing a U.S. Federal income tax return. See "Filing Requirements" in the IRS Form 1040 Filing Instructions to determine whether you were required to file.

For purposes of this affidavit, the line for gross (total) income on IRS Forms 1040 and 1040A will be considered when determining income. For persons filing IRS Form 1040 EZ, the line for adjusted gross income will be considered.

Obtaining Tax Transcripts. You may use Internal Revenue Service (IRS) Form 4506-T to request tax transcripts from the IRS. Complete IRS Form 4506-T with the ending date for each of your three most recent tax years listed on line 9. Follow all instructions for completing and filing Form 4506-T with the IRS.

Part 7. Use of Assets to Supplement Income.

Only complete this Part if you need to use the value of assets to meet the income requirements. If your Total Household Income (indicated on **Line 24c**) is equal to or more than needed to meet the income requirement as shown by the current Poverty Guidelines (Form I-864P) for your household size (indicated on **Line 21h**), you do not need to complete this Part. If your total household income does not meet the requirement, you may submit evidence of the value of your assets, the sponsored immigrant's assets, and/or assets of a household member that can be used, if necessary, for the support of the intending immigrant(s). The value of assets of all of these persons may be combined in order to meet the necessary requirement.

Only assets that can be converted into cash within one year and without considerable hardship or financial loss to the owner may be included. The owner of the asset must include a description of the asset, proof of ownership, and the basis for the owner's claim of its net cash value.

You may include the net value of your home as an asset. The net value of the home is the appraised value of the home, minus the sum of any and all loans secured by a mortgage, trust deed, or other lien on the home. If you wish to include the net value of your home, this, you must include documentation demonstrating that you own it, a recent appraisal by a licensed appraiser, and evidence of the amount of any and all loans secured by a mortgage, trust deed, or other lien on the home. You may not include the net value an automobile unless you show that you have more than one automobile, and at least one automobile is not included as an asset.

26. Assets.

To use your own assets, you must complete lines **26a** through **26d** and submit corresponding evidence with this form. Supporting evidence must be attached to establish location, ownership, date of acquisition, and value of any real estate holding.

27. Household Member's Assets.

To use the assets of a relative (spouse, adult son or daughter, parent or sibling), the relative must reside with you and have completed a Form I-864A, Contract Between Sponsor and Household Member, with accompanying evidence of assets. The Form I-864A and accompanying evidence of assets is submitted with Form I-864. You may use the assets of more than one relative who resides with you so long as you submit a complete Form I-864A with evidence of assets for each such relative.

28. Assets of the Intending Immigrant.

You may use the assets of the intending immigrant regardless of where he or she resides. The intending immigrant must provide evidence of such assets with this form. Form I-864A is not required to document the intending immigrant's assets.

29. Total Value of Assets.

In order to qualify based on the value of your assets, the total value of your assets must equal at least five times the difference between your total household income and the current poverty guidelines for your household size. However, if you are a U.S. citizen and you are sponsoring your spouse or minor child, the total value of your assets must only be equal to at least three times the difference. If the intending immigrant is an alien orphan who will be adopted in the United States after the alien orphan acquires permanent residence, and who will, as a result, acquire citizenship under section 320 of the Act, the total value of your assets need only equal the difference.

Example of How to Use Assets: If you are petitioning for a parent and the poverty line for your household size is $22,062 and your current income is $18,062, the difference between your current income and the poverty line is $4,000. In order for assets to help you qualify, the combination of your assets, plus the assets of any household member who is signing Form I-864A, plus any available assets of the sponsored immigrant, would have to equal five times this difference (5 x $4,000). In this case, you would meet the income requirements if the net value of the assets equaled at least $20,000.

Part 8. Sponsor's Contact.

Read the contract carefully, print your name, and then sign and date the form. **If you do not print your name on line 30 and sign and date the form on line 31, the intending immigrant you are sponsoring cannot be issued a visa or be granted adjustment of status.**

Other Information.

Penalties.

The Government may pursue verification of any information provided on or in support of this form, including employment, income, or assets with the employer, financial or other institutions, the Internal Revenue Service, or the Social Security Administration. If you include in this affidavit of support any information that you know to be false, you may be liable for criminal prosecution under the laws of the United States.

If you fail to give notice of your change of address, as required by 8 U.S.C. 1183a(d) and 8 CFR 213a.3, you may be liable for the civil penalty established by 8 U.S.C. 1183a(d)(2). The amount of the civil penalty will depend on whether you failed to give this notice because you were aware that the immigrant(s) you sponsored had received Federal, State, or local means-tested public benefits.

If the failure to report your change of address occurs with knowledge that the sponsored immigrant received means-tested public benefits (other than benefits described in section 401(b), 403(c)(2), or 4ll(b) of the Personal Responsibility and Work Opportunity Reconciliation Act of 1996, which are summarized in the contract in Part 8) such failure may result in a fine of not less than $2,000 or more than $5,000. Otherwise, the failure to report your change of address may result in a fine not less than $250 or more than $2,000.

Privacy Act Notice.

Authority for the collection of the information requested on this form is contained in 8 U.S.C. 1182a(4), 1183a, 1184(a), and 1258. The information will be used principally by an immigration judge, USCIS or a Consular Officer to support an alien's application for benefits under the Immigration and Nationality Act and specifically the assertion that he or she has adequate means of financial support and will not become a public charge. Submission of the information is voluntary. Failure to provide the information will result in denial of the application for an immigrant visa or adjustment of status.

The information may also, as a matter of routine use, be disclosed to other Federal, State and local agencies providing means-tested public benefits for use in civil action against the sponsor for breach of contract. Social Security numbers may be verified with the Social Security Administration consistant with the consent signed as part of the contract in **Part 8** of the Form I-864. It may also be disclosed as a matter of routine use to other Federal, State, local, and foreign law enforcement and regulatory agencies to enable these entities to carry out their law enforcement responsibilities.

USCIS Forms and Information.

To order USCIS forms, call our toll-free forms line at **1-800-870-3676.** You can also obtain forms and information on immigration laws, regulations and procedures by telephoning our National Customer Service Center at **1-800-375-5283** or visiting our internet website at **www.uscis.gov.**

Use InfoPass for Appointments.

As an alternative to waiting in line for assistance at your local USCIS office, you can now schedule an appointment through our internet-based system, **InfoPass**. To access the system, visit our website at **www.uscis.gov**. Use the **InfoPass** appointment scheduler and follow the screen prompts to set up your appointment. **InfoPass** generates an electronic appointment notice that appears on the screen. Print the notice and take it with you to your appointment. The notice gives the time and date of your appointment, along with the address of the USCIS office.

Reporting Burden.

A person is not required to respond to a collection of information unless it displays a currently valid OMB control number.

We try to create forms and instructions that are accurate, can be easily understood, and which impose the least burden on you to provide us with information. Often this is difficult because some immigration laws are very complex.

The estimated average time to complete and file this form is as follows: (1) 75 minutes to learn about the law and form; (2) 80 minutes to complete the form; and (3) 1 hour and 5 minutes to assemble and file the form; for a total estimated average of 4 hour and 30 minutes per form.

If you have comments regarding the accuracy of this estimate, or suggestions for making this form simpler, write to U.S. Citizenship and Immigration Services, Regulatory Management Division, Attn: OMB No. 1615-0075, 111 Massachusetts Avenue N.W., Washington, D.C. 20529. **Do not mail your completed affidavit of support to this address.**

Check List

The following items must be submitted with Form I-864:

For ALL sponsors:

____ A copy of your individual **Federal income tax return, including W-2s** for the most recent tax year, or a statement and/or evidence describing why you were not required to file. Also include a copy of each and every Form 1099, Schedule, and any other evidence of reported income. You may submit this information for the most recent three tax years , pay stub(s) from the most recent six months, and/or a letter from your employer if you believe any of these items will help you qualify.

For SOME sponsors:

____ **If you are currently self-employed**, a copy of your Schedule C, D, E or F from your most recent Federal Tax Return which establishes your income from your business.

____ If you are sponsoring more than one intending immigrant listed on the same affidavit of support, **photocopies of the original affidavit of support** may be submitted for any additional intending immigrants listed. Copies of supporting documentation are not required for these family members.

____ If you are the petitioning sponsor and on active duty in the U.S. Armed Forces and are sponsoring your spouse or child using 100 percent of governing poverty guideline, **proof of your active military status**.

____ If you are using the income of persons in your household or dependents to qualify,

    ____ A separate **Form I-864A** for each person whose income you will use. However, an intending immigrant whose income is being used needs to complete Form I-864A only if his or her spouse and/or children are immigrating with him or her.

    ____ Proof of their **residency in your household and relationship** to you if they are not the intending immigrants or are not listed as dependents on your Federal income tax return for the most recent tax year.

    ____ Proof that the intending immigrant's current employment **will continue from the same source** if his or her income is being used.

    ____ A copy of their individual **Federal income tax return, including W-2s and 1099s,** for the most recent tax year, or evidence that they were not required to file. You may submit this information for the most recent three years if you believe it will help you qualify.

____ If you use your assets or the assets of a household member to qualify,

    ____ Documentation of assets establishing location, ownership, date of acquisition and value. Evidence of any liens or liabilities against these assets.

    ____ A separate **Form I-864A** for each household member using assets other than for the intending immigrant.

____ If you are a joint sponsor, substitute sponsor, or the relative of an employment-based immigrant requiring an affidavit of support, **proof of your citizenship status, U.S. national status or lawful permanent resident status.**

    ____ For U.S. citizens or nationals, a copy of your birth certificate, passport, or certificate of naturalization or citizenship.

    ____ For lawful permanent residents, a copy of both sides of your Form I-551, Permanent Resident Card.

☐ District Court   ☐ Denver Juvenile Court

_____County, Colorado

Court Address:

IN THE MATTER OF THE PETITION OF:

FOR THE ADOPTION OF A CHILD

Attorney or Party Without Attorney (Name and Address):

Phone Number:

FAX Number:

E-mail:

Atty. Reg. #:

▲   **COURT USE ONLY**   ▲

Case Number:

Division   Courtroom

DECREE OF FOREIGN ADOPTION

This matter comes on for hearing this _____ day of _____, _____ upon petition of _____ seeking a decree declaring validation of an adoption granted by a court of competent jurisdiction of a country other than the United States of America. Petition filed in the District Court of _____ County on _____, _____ (date).

The Court having considered said petition and the evidence offered in support thereof, and being fully advised in the premises,

FINDS THAT: _____ adopting parent(s) is/are citizen(s) and resident(s) of the State of Colorado;

That the criminal records check of the prospective adoptive parent(s), as reported to the Court by the county department of social services, the designated qualified individual, the child placement agency or Petitioner does not reveal a criminal case.

The Court has examined the original or certified copy of a valid foreign adoption decree, together with the notarized translation, which have been presented to the court.

The child's name listed in the foreign adoption decree is _____.

The child is either a permanent resident or a naturalized citizen of the United States of America.

IT IS THEREFORE ORDERED THAT, pursuant to §19-5-205, C.R.S. as amended, the Court declares the decree granted by a court of competent jurisdiction in _____, as valid, and the decree issued this date shall have the same legal effect as any decree of adoption issued by this court.

The child's name is ordered changed to: _____.

DONE AND DATED: _____

BY THE COURT:

_____

Magistrate/Judge

JDF 524 8/00 DECREE OF FOREIGN ADOPTION

ADOPT-200 **Adoption Request**

Clerk stamps date here when form is filed.

If you are adopting more than one child, fill out an adoption request for each child.

(1) Your name (adopting parent):

a. _____

b. _____

Relationship to child: _____

Street address: _____

City: _____ State: _____ Zip: _____

Telephone number: (____) _____

Lawyer *(if any): (Name, address, telephone numbers, and State Bar number):*

_____

_____

_____

Fill in court name and street address:

Superior Court of California, County of

Fill in case number if known:

Case Number:

(2) Type of adoption *(check one):*

☐ Agency *(name):* _____

  ☐ Joinder has been filed.

  ☐ Joinder will be filed.

☐ Independent

☐ International *(name of agency):* _____

☐ Stepparent

☐ Relative

(3) Information about the child:

a. The child's new name will be:

_____

b. ☐ Boy ☐ Girl

c. Date of birth: _____ Age: _____

d. Child's address *(if different from yours):*

Street: _____

City: _____ State: ____ Zip: _____

e. Place of birth *(if known):*

City: _____

State: _____ Country: _____

f. If the child is 12 or older, does the child agree to the adoption? ☐ Yes ☐ No

g. Date child was placed in your physical care:

_____

(4) Child's name before adoption: *(Fill out ONLY if this is an independent, relative, or stepparent adoption.)*

_____

(5) Does the child have a legal guardian? ☐ Yes ☐ No

If yes, attach a copy of the Letters of Guardianship and fill out below:

a. Date guardianship ordered: _____

b. County: _____

c. Case number: _____

(6) Is the child a dependent of the court? ☐ Yes ☐ No

If yes, fill out below:

Juvenile case number: _____

County: _____

(To be completed by the clerk of the superior court if a hearing date is available.)

Hearing is set for:

Hearing → Date Date: _____

Time: _____

Dept.: _____ Room: _____

Name and address of court if different from above:

_____

To the person served with this request: If you do not come to this hearing, the judge can order the adoption without your input.

Judicial Council of California, www.courtinfo.ca.gov
Revised January 1, 2007, Mandatory Form
Family Code, §§ 8714, 8714.5, 8802, 8912, 9000; Welfare & Institutions Code, § 16119; Cal. Rules of Court, rule 5.730
Adoption Request
ADOPT-200, Page 1 of 3 →

246

Your name: _____

7 Child may have Indian ancestry: ☐ Yes ☐ No
If yes, attach Form ADOPT-220, Adoption of Possible Indian Child.

8 Names of birth parents, if known:
    a. Mother: _____
    b. Father: _____

9 **If this is an agency adoption**
    a. I have received information about the Adoption Assistance Program Regional Center and about mental health services available through Medi-Cal or other programs. ☐ Yes ☐ No
    b. All persons with parental rights agree that the child should be placed for adoption by the California Department of Social Services or a licensed adoption agency (Fam. Code, § 8700) and have signed a relinquishment form approved by the California Department of Social Services. ☐ Yes ☐ No *(if no, list the name and relationship to child of each person who has not signed the consent form):* _____
_____

10 **If this is an independent adoption**
    a. A copy of the Independent Adoptive Placement Agreement, a California Department of Social Services form, is attached. (This is required in most independent adoptions; see Fam. Code, § 8802.)
    b. All persons with parental rights agree to the adoption and have signed the Independent Adoptive Placement Agreement, a California Department of Social Services form. ☐ Yes ☐ No *(if no, list the name and relationship to child of each person who has not signed the consent form):* _____
_____

    c. I will file promptly with the department or delegated county adoption agency the information required by the department in the investigation of the proposed adoption.

11 **If this is a stepparent adoption**
    a. The birth parent *(name):* _____ ☐ has signed a consent ☐ will sign a consent
    b. The birth parent *(name):* _____ ☐ has signed a consent ☐ will sign a consent
    c. The adopting parents were married on **or** The domestic partnership was registered on *(date):* _____. *(For court use only. This does not affect social worker's recommendation. There is no waiting period.)*

12 ☐ There is no presumed or biological father because the child was conceived by artificial insemination, using semen provided to a medical doctor or a sperm bank. (Fam. Code, § 7613.)

13 **Contact after adoption**
Form ADOPT-310, *Contact After Adoption Agreement,* ☐ is attached ☐ will not be used ☐ will be filed at least 30 days before the adoption hearing ☐ is undecided at this time

14 ☐ The consent of the ☐ birth mother ☐ presumed father is not necessary because *(specify Fam. Code, § 8606 subdivision):* _____

Case Number:

Your name: _____

(15) A court ended the parental rights of *(attach copy of order):*

Name: _____ Relationship to child: _____ on *(date)*_____

Name: _____ Relationship to child: _____ on *(date)*_____

(16) ☐ I will ask the court to end the parental rights of *(attach copy of Petition to Terminate Parental Rights or Freedom From Parental Custody, if filed):*

Name: _____ Relationship to child: _____

Name: _____ Relationship to child: _____

(17) Each of the following persons with parental rights has not contacted his or her child in one year or more. *(Fam. Code, § 8604(b))* (Attach copy of Application for Freedom From Parental Custody, if filed.)

Name: _____ Relationship to child: _____

Name: _____ Relationship to child: _____

(18) Each of the following persons with parental rights has died:

Name: _____ Relationship to child: _____

Name: _____ Relationship to child: _____

(19) **Suitability for adoption**
Each adopting parent:

  a. Is at least 10 years older than the child   d. Has a suitable home for the child *and*

  b. Will treat the child as his or her own   e. Agrees to adopt the child

  c. Will support and care for the child

(20) I ask the court to approve the adoption and to declare that the adopting parents and the child have the legal relationship of parent and child, with all the rights and duties of this relationship, including the right of inheritance.

(21) If a lawyer is representing you in this case, he or she must sign here:

Date: _____   _____   ▶ _____
                    Type or print your name   *Signature of attorney for adopting parents*

(22) I declare under penalty of perjury under the laws of the State of California that the information in this form is true and correct to my knowledge. This means that if I lie on this form, I am guilty of a crime.

Date: _____   _____   ▶ _____
                    Type or print your name   *Signature of adopting parent*

Date: _____   _____   ▶ _____
                    Type or print your name   *Signature of adopting parent*

FL-200

ATTORNEY OR PARTY WITHOUT ATTORNEY *(Name, state bar number, and address)*:	FOR COURT USE ONLY
TELEPHONE NO. *(Optional)*:　　　　FAX NO. *(Optional)*:	
E-MAIL ADDRESS *(Optional)*:	
ATTORNEY FOR *(Name)*:	

SUPERIOR COURT OF CALIFORNIA, COUNTY OF
　STREET ADDRESS:
　MAILING ADDRESS:
　CITY AND ZIP CODE:
　BRANCH NAME:

PETITIONER:

RESPONDENT:

PETITION TO ESTABLISH PARENTAL RELATIONSHIP ☐ Child Support ☐ Child Custody ☐ Visitation ☐ Other *(specify)*:	CASE NUMBER:

1. Petitioner is
　a. ☐ the mother.
　b. ☐ the father.
　c. ☐ the child or the child's personal representative *(specify court and date of appointment)*:
　d. ☐ other *(specify)*:

2. The children are
　a. <u>Child's name</u>　　　　　　　<u>Date of birth</u>　　　<u>Age</u>　　　　<u>Sex</u>

　b. ☐ a child who is not yet born.

3. The court has jurisdiction over the respondent because the respondent
　a. ☐ resides in this state.
　b. ☐ had sexual intercourse in this state, which resulted in conception of the children listed in item 2.
　c. ☐ other *(specify)*:

4. The action is brought in this county because *(you must check one or more to file in this county)*:
　a. ☐ the child resides or is found in the county.
　b. ☐ a parent is deceased and proceedings for administration of the estate have been or could be started in this county.

5. Petitioner claims *(check all that apply)*:
　a. ☐ respondent is the child's mother.
　b. ☐ respondent is the child's father.
　c. ☐ parentage has been established by Voluntary Declaration of Paternity *(attach copy)*.
　d. ☐ respondent who is child's parent has failed to support the child.
　e. ☐ *(name)*:　　　　　　　　　　　　　has furnished or is furnishing the following reasonable expenses
　　　of pregnancy and birth for which the respondent as parent of the child is obligated:
　　　<u>Amount</u>　　　　<u>Payable to</u>　　　　　　　<u>For *(specify)*</u>:

　f. ☐ public assistance is being provided to the child.
　g. ☐ other *(specify)*:

6. A completed *Declaration Under Uniform Child Custody Jurisdiction and Enforcement Act (UCCJEA))* (form FL-105) is attached.

Form Approved for Optional Use
Judicial Council of California
FL-200 [Rev. January 1, 2003]

PETITION TO ESTABLISH PARENTAL RELATIONSHIP
(Uniform Parentage)

Family Code, § 7630
www.courtinfo.ca.gov

PETITIONER:	CASE NUMBER:
RESPONDENT:	

Petitioner requests the court to make the determinations indicated below.

7. PARENT-CHILD RELATIONSHIP
   a. ☐ Respondent   b. ☐ Petitioner
   c. ☐ Other *(specify):*   is the parent of the children listed in item 2.

8. CHILD CUSTODY AND VISITATION   Petitioner   Respondent   Joint   Other
   a. Legal custody of children to   ☐   ☐   ☐   ☐
   b. Physical custody of children to   ☐   ☐   ☐   ☐
   c. Visitation of children:
      (1) ☐ None
      (2) ☐ Reasonable visitation.
      (3) ☐ Petitioner ☐ Respondent   should have the right to visit the children as follows:

      (4) ☐ Visitation with the following restrictions *(specify):*

   d. Facts in support of the requested custody and visitation orders are *(specify):*
      ☐ Contained in the attached declaration.
   e. ☐ I request mediation to work out a parenting plan.

9. REASONABLE EXPENSES OF PREGNANCY AND BIRTH:
  Reasonable expenses of pregnancy   Petitioner   Respondent   Joint
  and birth be paid by   ☐   ☐   ☐
  as follows:

10. FEES AND COSTS OF LITIGATION   Petitioner   Respondent   Joint
   a. Attorney fees to be paid by   ☐   ☐   ☐
   b. Expert fees, guardian ad litem fees, and other costs   ☐   ☐   ☐
      of the action or pretrial proceedings to be paid by

11. NAME CHANGE
   ☐ Children's names be changed, according to Family Code section 7638, as follows *(specify):*

12. CHILD SUPPORT
   The court may make orders for support of the children and issue an earnings assignment without further notice to either party.

13. I have read the restraining order on the back of the *Summons* (FL-210) and I understand it applies to me when this Petition is filed.

I declare under penalty of perjury under the laws of the State of California that the foregoing is true and correct.

Date:

▶

_____   _____
(TYPE OR PRINT NAME)   (SIGNATURE OF PETITIONER)

A blank *Response to Petition to Establish Parental Relationship* (form FL-220) must be served on the Respondent with this Petition.

> NOTICE: If you have a child from this relationship, the court is required to order child support based upon the income of both parents. Support normally continues until the child is 18. You should supply the court with information about your finances. Otherwise, the child support order will be based upon information supplied by the other parent. Any party required to pay child support must pay interest on overdue amounts at the "legal" rate, which is currently 10 percent.

FL-200 [Rev. January 1, 2003]   **PETITION TO ESTABLISH PARENTAL RELATIONSHIP**   Page 2 of 2
                                       (Uniform Parentage)

F.C.A. § 661;
S.C.P.A. §§ 1701 - 1704

Form 6-1
(Petition for Appointment
of Guardianship of a
Person)
(9/2006)

....

Proceeding for the Appointment of a
Guardian of the Person

Docket No.

                        of

                  a Minor

PETITION
(Appointment of
Guardian of Person)

....

TO THE FAMILY COURT:

The Petitioner respectfully alleges to this Court that:

1. The name and domicile of the Petitioner are as follows:
(State name and address, including street, city, village or town, county and state)

2. The name, date of birth and domicile of the child subject to this proceeding are as follows:

Name:
Date of Birth:
Address of the child [include street, city, village or town, county and state]:

3. The subject child ☐ is ☐ is not a Native American child subject to the *Indian Child Welfare Act of 1978* (25 U.S.C. §§ 1901-1963). If so, the following have been notified [check applicable box(es)]:
☐ parent/custodian [specify name and give notification date]:
☐ tribe/nation [specify name and give notification date]:
☐ United States Secretary of the Interior [give notification date]:

4. The residence of the child and relationship of person with whom the child resides are as follows:

Person with whom child resides [specify name]:
Relationship to child:
Address [include street, city, village or town, county and state]:

Form 6-1 page 2

5. (Upon information and belief) The religion of the child is

6. The names, relationship and post office addresses of the parents of the child, the name and address of the person with whom the child resides, if other than the parent(s), on whom process should issue; and such other persons concerning whom the court is required to have information, are as follows:(If either parent is dead, so allege; if both parents are dead, include nearest adult next to kin who is a domiciliary.)

Relationship   Name   Post Office Address [include street, city, village or
                                                              town, county and state]

Mother:
Father:
Person with whom
  the child resides, if other
  than parents:
Other [specify]: [1]

7. To protect and preserve the legal rights of the child, it is necessary that some proper person be duly appointed the guardian of (his)(her) person, because:

8. (Upon information and belief) No guardian pursuant to will or deed, or guardian of the person pursuant to Section 384 or 384-b of the Social Services Law, has been previously appointed for the child except:

9 (a). Upon information and belief, the person nominated to be a guardian herein is not the subject of an indicated report, as such term is defined in Section 412 of the Social Services Law, filed with the statewide register of child abuse and maltreatment pursuant to Title Six of Article Six of the Social Services Law. If the person is the subject of such a report, specify the_date, status and circumstances to the extent known:

_____ (b). Upon information and belief, the person nominated to be a guardian herein is not the subject of or the respondent in a child protective proceeding commenced under Article Ten of the Family Court Act. If the person is the subject of such a proceeding, specify whether the proceeding resulted in an order finding that the child is an abused or neglected child, and provide the date and status to the extent known:

---

[1]Include Mental Hygiene Legal Services if the child is a mentally retarded or developmentally disabled person admitted to a facility.

Form 6-1 page 3

(c). Upon information and belief, the person nominated to be a guardian herein is not the subject of an Order of Protection or Temporary Order of Protection in any criminal, matrimonial or Family Court proceeding(s). If such an order has been issued, specify the court, docket or index number, date of order, expiration date of order, next court date and status of case to the extent known:

10 (a). The following adults who are age 18 or older live in the home of the proposed guardian:

Name   Relationship, if any, to the child   Date of Birth

(b). Upon information and belief,[check applicable box]: □none of the above adults □the following adult(s)[specify]:   )
(is)(are) the subject of an indicated report, as such term is defined in Section 412 of the Social Services Law, filed with the statewide register of child abuse and maltreatment pursuant to Title Six of Article Six of the Social Services Law. If so, specify_____date, status and circumstances to the extent known:

(c). Upon information and belief,[check applicable box]: □none of the above adults □the following adult(s)[specify]:
(has) (have) been the subject of or the Respondent in a child protective proceeding commenced under Article 10 of the Family Court Act. If so, specify whether proceeding resulted in an order finding that the child is an abused or neglected child, date and status to the extent known:

(d). Upon information and belief, an Order of Protection or Temporary Order of Protection □has □has not been issued against any of the above adults. If such an order has been issued in any criminal, matrimonial or Family Court proceeding(s), specify the adult against whom the order was issued, the court that issued the order, docket or index number, date of order, expiration date of order, next court date and status of case, if available:

11. The person nominated to be the guardian has consented to the appointment, a copy of which is attached.[2]

---

[2]If petitioner is applying for letters of guardianship on behalf of another.

Form 6-1 page 4

12.   , parent(s) of the child, although living, should not be
appointed guardian of the person of the child because:

13. [Applicable where the child is 18 years of age or older; delete if inapplicable]:
The child, who is over the age of 21, has consented to the appointment of the guardian, a copy
of which is attached.

14. There are no persons interested in this proceeding other than those mentioned
above.

15. No prior application has been made to any court for the relief requested herein .

WHEREFORE, Petitioner requests that an order be entered appointing
to be the guardian of the person of the child until the child reaches the age of 21 and that letters
of guardianship issue.

Dated: _____

                                          Signature of Petitioner

                                          _____

                                          Print or type name

                                          _____

_____   Signature of Attorney, if any

                                          _____

_____   Attorney' s Name (Print or Type)

                                          _____

_____
_____   Attorney' s Address and Telephone Number

_____   VERIFICATION

STATE OF NEW YORK   )
)ss.:
COUNTY OF   )
                                 ,being duly sworn, says that (s)he is the Petitioner in the
above-named proceeding and that the foregoing petition is true to (his)(her) own knowledge, except as to matters
therein stated to be alleged on information and belief and as to those matters (s)he believes it to be true.

Sworn to before me this
day of   .

                                          _____

                                                    Petitioner

_____
(Deputy)Clerk of the Court
    Notary Public

PETITION FOR COURT APPROVAL OF STANDBY GUARDIAN

Commonwealth of Virginia   VA. CODE § 16.1-350, 16.1-352

Case No.: _____

_____ Juvenile and Domestic Relations District Court

In re _____ , a child under eighteen years of age

_____
PETITIONER

_____
RELATIONSHIP OF PETITIONER TO CHILD

_____
ADDRESS

_____
CHILD'S ADDRESS

_____
CHILD'S DATE OF BIRTH

PARENTS

_____
NAME OF FATHER

_____
NAME OF MOTHER

_____
ADDRESS

_____
ADDRESS

☐ Father ☐ Mother is the qualified parent.

PROPOSED/DESIGNATED STANDBY GUARDIAN

_____
NAME OF PROPOSED/DESIGNATED STANDBY GUARDIAN

_____
ALTERNATE PROPOSED STANDBY GUARDIAN

_____
ADDRESS

_____
ADDRESS

☐ **APPROVAL OF PROPOSED STANDBY GUARDIAN**

1. The Petitioner requests that _____ be approved as the standby guardian
NAME OF PROPOSED STANDBY GUARDIAN

   for _____ and _____
   NAME OF CHILD   NAME OF ALTERNATE STANDBY GUARDIAN
   be approved as the alternate.

2. The Petitioner requests that the standby guardian be given authority as a ☐ guardian of the person and/or ☐ guardian of the property of the minor.

3. ☐ There is a significant risk that the qualified parent will imminently become physically or mentally incapable of caring for the child or die as a result of a progressive chronic condition or illness. It is not necessary for the Petitioner to produce medical records to establish this condition at the time of filing of the petition.

4. The proposed triggering event is receipt by the standby guardian of a ☐ determination of incompetence or certificate of death, whichever is earlier; OR ☐ written consent of the qualified parent and filing of the consent with the Court upon the following conditions:

_____

☐ **APPROVAL OF A DESIGNATED STANDBY GUARDIAN**

1. ☐ A copy of the written designation of ＿＿＿＿＿＿＿＿＿＿＿＿＿＿ as standby guardian for
NAME OF STANDBY GUARDIAN

＿＿＿＿＿＿＿＿＿＿＿＿ by ＿＿＿＿＿＿＿＿＿＿＿＿＿＿
NAME OF CHILD   NAME OF QUALIFIED PARENT
is attached.

2. The authority of the designated standby guardian has been triggered by

☐ A determination of incompetence. A copy of the determination is attached.
☐ The death of the qualified parent. A copy of the death certificate is attached.
☐ A determination of debilitation and written consent by the qualified parent to commencement of the authority of the standby guardian. A copy of the determination and the written consent is attached.

☐ A determination of incompetence or debilitation has been made. Determination was made on ＿＿＿＿＿＿ by
DATE

＿＿＿＿＿＿＿＿＿＿＿＿＿＿
NAME OF PHYSICIAN

The qualified parent's attending physician is:

＿＿＿＿＿＿＿＿＿＿＿＿＿＿＿＿＿＿＿＿＿
NAME AND ADDRESS OF ATTENDING PHYSICIAN

Reasons why the child's other parent is not assuming or should not assume the responsibilities of a standby guardian are:

There ☐ is ☐ is not any prior judicial history regarding custody of the child or any pending litigation regarding custody of the child. If so, please provide details and case number, if known:

＿＿＿＿＿＿＿＿＿＿＿＿   ＿＿＿＿＿＿＿＿＿＿＿＿＿＿
DATE   PETITIONER

The Petitioner appeared this date before the undersigned and, upon being duly sworn, made oath that the facts stated in the foregoing petition are true based on the Petitioner's knowledge.

＿＿＿＿＿＿＿＿＿＿＿＿＿＿＿＿   ＿＿＿＿＿＿＿＿＿＿＿＿＿＿
DATE   ☐ CLERK   ☐ INTAKE OFFICER
                        ☐ NOTARY PUBLIC (MY COMMISSION EXPIRES ＿＿＿＿＿＿＿.

Index

About the Author

Brette McWhorter Sember received her J.D. from the State University of New York at Buffalo and practiced in New York state before retiring to become a writer. She is the author of more than thirty books, including how to *Parent with Your Ex: Working Together for Your Child's Best Interest, The Infertility Answer Book, Gay & Lesbian Parenting Choices, Your Plus-Size Pregnancy, Your Practical Pregnancy, The Divorce Organizer & Planner, No-Fight Divorce* and many more. She is a member of ASJA (American Society of Journalist and Authors) and AHCJ (Association of Health Care Journalists). She is the recipient of the 1999 Media Award from Family and Home Network (formerly Mothers at Home).

Sember has extensive training in cases involving children and was on the Law Guardian panel in three counties. Her practice included adoptions, which she found to be the happiest cases to take place in Family Court. She is also a trained family mediator and is experienced in a wide variety of family issues. Children have always been her main focus throughout her career. Sember currently provides services as a custody coach, providing support, information, and assistance to parents going through custody cases.

Sember writes and speaks often about children and family. Her work has appeared in over 170 magazines including *Conceive, Pregnancy, ePregnancy, Fit Pregnancy, American Baby, Single Mother Magazine,* and many others. She is the mother of two children.